Empower Your~~~

"It's a classic tale: we want to change but don't know how. For anyone who has tried countless fads, expensive therapists and a myriad of spiritual mumbo-jumbo books, Richard Walker will be your new hero and best friend. His book breaks down in easy accessible steps how to implement change in your life, to make you a better happier person. **Simple, yet life changing for those who are ready to stop being a victim** and be happy to be alive. Richard is an inspiration. Thank you."

Jessica Henning
Bond Girl Bootcamp
www.BondGirlBootcamp.com

"**I love it, must read!** A simple approach to life that anyone can make their own, which for me means that I now happily eat cherry tomatoes. It just takes practice."

Shelli Taylor
RVP Starbucks, China

"I have been clean off drugs for several years and have achieved this through a 12 step program. The program requires changing how I have been reacting to the issues life brings. I have had to make a lot of changes in my behavior. As issues come up I attempt to react/act differently, in a positive way instead of the self destructive behaviors I have learned over the years. This book was given to me, to help me do a deeper evaluation into the negative beliefs I created that are preventing me from putting my thoughts of change into action. The *changing of beliefs has proven to be very effective.* **It has worked so well for me** *that I have shared this process with my support group so they can benefit."*

Susan Gutierrez
Efficient Technology, Inc.
www.EfficientTech.com

"Richard Walker is one of the most inspiring people I know and **this book will change lots of lives** *- hopefully yours! Richard really breaks down some powerful ideas into simple and practical steps to help you retrain your mind. He's a living example that it works."*

Aaron Ross
PebbleStorm
www.UniqueGenius.com

"I often put off losing weight because I feel like becoming skinnier makes me not enough...literally. I'm petite and small boned and repeatedly choose not to lose weight, because of my feelings of becoming skinny get mixed in with not-'enoughness'. The extra weight makes me feel more substantial. Going through the steps of understanding why and choosing different thoughts/perspectives was the first stop in getting more fit and healthy. Thanks Richard Walker! **Your book made a huge difference!** *I am of course more than enough at any size!"*

Onna Young
www.LifeAfterDebt.us

"When I picked up this book **I had no idea it would transform my life!** Approaching middle age, I felt I had let go of something important to me, and with the help of this book, I was able to substantiate the spiritual and emotional cost of losing something dear to me. In doing the simple, yet effective exercises in the book, I was able to clearly see the path towards regaining the pieces that fulfill me and make me more complete. Since my initial breakthrough, I have gone back again and worked on other areas focusing my lens on what balance means for me. I am grateful for picking up Richard's book. I hope you have a similar journey as you start examining places where you feel you might be stuck. **This book will give you that nudge** and give you focus on how to transform your life too."

Marylou Tyler
Telegenik Communications
www.telegenik.com

"**This is an easy-to-read guide everyone can get something out of.** The steps are easy to follow and are things anyone can do without spending many years and lots of money on counseling or therapy. Sometimes just knowing the right question can change your life and this book provides a way of getting to those questions and examining the answers. If you're struggling with a decision or bad habits or know you're not happy but you don't know why, then this is a must read."

Cheryl Dillon
Artist, Editor and Consultant

"At first I thought the book "It's My Life! I Can Change If I Want To" was too small to give me growth in a personal way. I have usually read books that have quite a few more chapters to feel like I was getting something out of them. After reading this book I realized a few things about myself and the way I have made choices that may or may not have worked for me. Then I really appreciated that it was enough to open up a discussion with myself about what I have in my life that I like and what I would like to change because of my beliefs from my past."

Lui Rodriguez
Lui's Hair Studio
www.LuisHairStudio.com

IT'S MY LIFE!

I Can Change If I Want To

Unlock Your Beliefs

Design Your Reality

Become Your Best Self

Richard D. Walker

It's My Life! I Can Change If I Want To

ISBN: 978-0-578-07421-4

Publisher: Richard D. Walker, Efficient Technology Inc.

Copyright © 2007 - 2011 Richard Walker. All rights reserved. No portion of this book may be reproduced mechanically, electronically, or by any other means, including photocopying, without written permission of the publisher. It is illegal to copy this book, post it to a website, or distribute it by any other means without permission from the publisher.

Richard Walker
Efficient Technology, Inc.
(877) 456-7845
Email: rwalker@RichardDWalker.com
www.RichardDWalker.com

Limits of Liability and Disclaimer of Warranty

The author and publisher shall not be liable for your misuse of this material. This book is strictly for information and educational purposes.

Warning – Disclaimer

The purpose of this book is to educate and entertain. The author and/or publisher do not guarantee that anyone following these techniques, suggestions, tips, ideas, strategies or examples will become successful. The author and/or publisher shall have neither liability nor responsibility to anyone with respect to any loss or damage caused, or alleged to be caused, directly or indirectly by the information contained in this book.

Contents

Introduction — 15

1 - Everything You Need To Know — 25

2 – Step 1: Desire To Change — 39

3 – Step 2: Believe You Can Change — 57

4 – Step 3: Unlock Your Beliefs — 79

5 – Step 4: Design Your Reality — 93

6 – The Victim's Roadblock To Change — 109

Conclusion – Become Your Best Self — 125

Appendix – A Fully Explained Example — 129

*This book is dedicated to you, the reader.
May you become your best version of yourself.*

Foreword

Awhile back my son presented me with what has turned out to be one of the greatest gifts of my life--a pre-publication copy of his book, "It's My Life! I Can Change If I Want To". Not only does he share the story of an integral part of our relationship as father and son, he explains how he developed an approach to life that helped him deal with adversity and affect desired change. I am sorry for my part in contributing to my son's pain, but I am grateful for how he learned to deal with change and challenge.

Recently I have been going through one of the most difficult times of my life and this book has been one of my guides--the chapter "The Victim's Roadblock To Change" has been especially helpful. Instead of allowing myself to feel like a victim to unexpected changes that threatened my business, I looked for what I had control over and began to do what I could do. Presently there seems to be a positive resolution, but no matter the outcome I now have a renewed confidence and tools to deal with change and adversity.

Richard skillfully interweaves his own story with very clear and detailed explanations of how to affect positive change. I believe every reader will find "It's My Life! I Can Change If I Want To" offers a wealth of strategies and tools to live a more fulfilling and rewarding life.

Harry Walker
New Insights Programs

Acknowledgements

I never thought I would write a book until I witnessed someone close to me go through the most difficult and painful time of their life. While I could not change what they went through I wanted to at least share my method for deriving strength, peace and happiness from the most challenging of situations. Suffice it to say, that person's pain inspired me to take action to write this book in the hopes they might glean even one insight to help them through their difficult time. I know I can't change anyone except myself, but nobody said we couldn't share our tools for changing.

With deep appreciation, I am grateful to my mother, father, brother, sister and aunts and uncles for being incredibly strong, supportive and positive influences throughout my entire life. I am thankful for my fiancé, for the incredible support and always positive encouragement she's shown me and my effort to complete this book. Thanks to my friends and colleagues who took the time to give me critical feedback and support I needed to make this book the best it can be.

Special thanks to Cheryl Dillon as editor of this book and Steven Walker for the cover artwork and artistic guidance.

Happiness is a choice

It's My Life!
I Can Change If I Want To

Introduction

You can't change the facts, only your attitude

Not too long ago my mother asked me, "Do you think you can change yourself?". It's an honest question that I think we all ask ourselves at some point, or at least we think about in regards to someone we'd like to change. Not only do I know people can change themselves, I have personally made long-lasting changes many times throughout my life and continue to change and evolve daily. Since age twelve I have been using a straight-forward and highly effective method I developed to affect long-lasting changes.

I call my method of change 'reprogramming my brain' because that is exactly what this method does. In my professional career I design software and architect enterprise technology solutions, so the concept of programming is very natural to me. If you've never dealt with software programming, it's a lot like writing a poem or baking a pie. Writing a poem requires that you write words and phrases in a common structure called a stanza and then order the lines and stanzas in just the right way to create an emotional effect in the reader. Baking a pie is also similar because you must mix ingredients together in the right way and in the right order and then cook the pie at just the right temperature if you want your pie to turn out great. Our brains work in a similar manner through a set of rules and logical structures that result in our behaviors and how we experience the world.

Although we might all ask ourselves how to change, most of us don't actually know a simple, straight-forward way to do it. I do and I want to share it with you. I know there are hundreds of other books on this topic because I have read many of them. I have the greatest respect for the doctors, psychologists and researchers who wrote their wonderful books. Their books have definitely helped me understand myself and evolve in ways I wouldn't have otherwise. But most of those books deal with specific types of problems or specific types of changes and they all have a different manner to achieve the changes they recommend.

This book is different. By reading this book you will learn a methodology for change that can be applied to any type of change, including the ones offered in other books. **This is the one book you should read if you want to create deep, long-lasting changes within yourself.** This book teaches you what you need to know in order to make the most of all the other books.

Whenever I have read a book on changing, whether it was on how to stop being a co-dependent, how to build wealth, or how to communicate better, there has always been one lesson missing: the exact steps to actually perform the change. Again, I'm reminded of a similarity with programming software: if you've ever read a book on how to write software (and if you haven't, you're probably glad!), then you might have noticed that authors typically assume you already know how software programming works. This book does not assume you already know how to change yourself, but it does assume you are or will become sufficiently interested in how you work in order to carry out changes and gain a firm understanding of who you are at your core.

What this methodology does is give you a way to directly access your beliefs and thoughts, and choose to change yourself as the result. You'll find that this book is relatively short and written in such a way that you can learn everything you need in the first chapter alone. Why should you spend the next four weeks reading before you learn how to change? Isn't that like reading 300 pages about basketball technique before even picking up a ball? **Read chapter one and you'll learn everything you need to know in order to start making changes today!**

Change Can Be Easy

I have heard a lot of different ways to change. Most people take a brute-force approach to change – "just use your willpower to do it and then keep doing it". That approach takes an inordinate amount of strength, drive and determination. Anyone can quit smoking for a day, but not just anyone can stop for a week or a month through force of mind alone. What if you don't have the willpower to stick with the change? What if there are forces within you that drive you back to the old behavior regardless of how strong your will is? If you rely on brute-force and fail, then you lose and sink lower into your old ways.

The methodology in this book is designed to help you make strong, lasting decisions that are easy to enforce and follow through with regardless of your willpower. Using this methodology will not require super-human willpower. Instead I use tools that are definitely within everyone's abilities. Reprogramming your brain only requires that you make simple, independent decisions that turn into real, permanent changes. You're going to find that change can be easy when you have a standard approach and toolset that is easy to understand and use.

How Powerful Is This Method?

When I originally told my sister about this methodology and how I used it in my mid-twenties to learn to like olives and mushrooms, she suggested that I write a book and title it "Life Is Too Short Not To Like Olives And Mushrooms". As much as I love cooking, this book isn't about cooking or even learning to like foods. It's about the power of the mind and how to harness that power through a structured approach to working with your brain.

Have you ever overcome a food you didn't like? Most of us in Western societies didn't grow up eating sushi so how did people come to like them? It could be that they never had a negative experience with sushi that caused them to reject it out of hand. It could also be that their only negative exposure was based on what their parents or peers said, and not on their own first-hand experience. Or it could even be that someone had a negative association with Japanese culture. In all these cases and many more, the reasons people may not like sushi are conditions of their mind and beliefs and may not be based on a physical reason like allergies.

Where do you draw your sense of happiness from? What's holding you back from achieving your definition of success? What can you do to become the person you envisioned when you were a child with dreams and ambitions? If happiness is derived from meeting your expectations, of achieving your definition of success, then **what you can do** to become the person of your own dreams **is change yourself**. The *ONLY* person who can change you is you. This book can help. My goal in writing this book is to empower you to become your best version of yourself. I don't know all the answers and I too am constantly learning. I hope to learn with you and hear how you overcame a challenge you faced. As you read and discover new ways to reprogram your mind towards your goals, please reach out to me and share your stories.

Life Is Too Short To Not Like Fish

I have successfully used my methodology to completely change how I feel about certain foods, which is quite powerful when you consider all the factors involved with food (taste, texture, physiological reactions, childhood reactions, etc.). My first attempt at using this methodology with food was when I started changing how I felt about fish.

From childhood until my mid-20's I didn't like fish. There were certain types of mild, white fish that I liked ok, but no matter how much I liked the taste, eight to ten bites would result in immediate nausea. At age 25 I went on a deep sea fishing trip to catch Dorado (Mahi Mahi). I decided at that point in time that if I was going to catch these fish that I better take part in eating them, which meant that I needed to stop feeling nausea. But I didn't just plug my nose or smother the fish in spices in order to 'learn' to like them. Rather, I made a conscious effort to change my beliefs and behavior towards eating fish. The results were so powerful that not only do I love fish and eat it every week my favorite way to eat fish is Sashimi style (raw cuts of fish).

Since I can change my physiological reactions to food (i.e. I no longer get nauseas when eating fish), then I know I can change anything about myself using my methodology. You can too. My method for changing is very straight-forward and designed to allow you to change on your own terms, for your own reasons and benefits, and on your time schedule. You'll find a lot of examples of how this methodology can be used, including how I have re-programmed myself to enjoy both olives and mushrooms.

Change Is The Only Constant

In life, the only change that's easy to make is getting four quarters for a dollar. Changes to your beliefs, your behaviors, your habits and your very nature are inherently difficult. The more you change, the easier it becomes, but it never becomes easy and you always have to put forth the effort to change if you want to change.

I have done a lot of traveling over the years and often meet new people, which often brings up the question, "Where are you from?". That's actually a difficult question to answer, so here's my story...

By the time I was 30 I had moved 29 times. I was born in Hamilton, Toronto, Canada and have dual citizenship with Canada and the US. My parents are both US citizens who were living in Canada at the time of my birth. Since my birth, I moved almost every year of my life, sometimes multiple times in a year. In addition to two provinces in Canada, I have lived in Southern California, Northern California, Reno, Las Vegas, Salt Lake City and Chicago.

The next question I get is, "Were your parents in the military?". No, we moved for different reasons. We moved for spiritual reasons, financial reasons, marital reasons, vocational reasons, and even to escape abusive people. I have lived in houses, apartments, condos, townhouses, a mobile home and even a hotel for a year and a half.

Needless to say, I have been through an enormous amount of change in moving alone. Throughout this book I relate several stories about my childhood and personal history and you'll see that I went through a lot before I turned 18. Since 18 I have been through even more changes including long-term relationships, moving every year, holding and losing different jobs, pursuing three careers and dealing with other serious life challenges and traumas.

I know change. In the first 35 years of my life, I went through more changes than most people go through in their entire lifetime. I will tell you that even after all these experiences, change is still not easy. Every time I move I know exactly what's going to happen, approximately how many items I own that will be lost or damaged in the move, how long it will take to pack, how long to move and unpack, how difficult it can be to get acclimated to the new neighborhood, etc. Knowing things are going to break doesn't make me any less upset when I unpack something that's broken. It is knowing how to change, knowing the process of change, that makes it easier to go through the event and to be more prepared to deal with the ups and downs.

By the end of this book you will have clear expectations about the process of change, but the actual change you make may still be challenging. It's like going to the gym: you dread going because you know how hard the workout is, but you go anyway because you want the results. Regardless of the type of change you attempt, it helps to recognize that there is going to be a certain amount of discomfort, awkwardness and pain.

Getting Through The Change Process

The most difficult obstacle to overcome when changing is our own fear of change itself. We fear what we don't know, whether we'll succeed or fail, whether we're taking the right course of action. Reprogramming your brain addresses these fears by design. The first step in the process, creating a desire to change, automatically addresses your fear of change. You don't have to look at your fear of change directly when you're riding on the strength of your desire to change. The second step, to believe you can change, overcomes that fear of change because you will believe you can succeed regardless of whether you fear the change or not.

The other type of fear we need to overcome is the fear of the actual process and how difficult that process will be. This fear is eliminated too because, by using this process, you know exactly how the process of change works. You know that if you spend the time assessing your beliefs and choosing to change those beliefs that you'll be making the changes you desire and fulfilling the belief that you can change.

NOTE: This Book Requires Exercise!

Like all goals and lessons in life, be prepared to make an effort if you want results. Reprogramming your mind requires performing distinct steps in a process to achieve the outcome you want. While the first chapter of this book tells you everything you need to know to make the life-long changes you want, the remaining chapters are more like exercises that will teach you a method and practice of how to make changes within yourself. The more experienced you become with these methods, the faster you can achieve results, but you need to start with the foundation of writing down your thoughts and measuring your results while reading this book.

Chapter 1

I can do anything I set my mind to

Everything You Need To Know

This method is for you and you alone. You cannot change others with this book, but they can change themselves by using the tools in this book. The key to making change is to make it for your own benefit and for your own reasons, which means that nobody else's reasons can cause you to change, nor can your reasons cause others to change.

This method is intended for anyone who wants to make choices for themselves. I personally started making self-aware changes when I was 12, beginning with my beliefs about spirituality. I'm not suggesting you give this book to your 12 year old, but it can be a powerful tool for anyone from teenagers to seniors. Anyone can change if they have the right tools.

How To Change

Reprogramming your brain is a four-step process and you can do these steps over any amount of time you may need, as long as you do all the steps in their correct order. What this process allows you to do is change the beliefs that create your behavior. With the right beliefs in place, any result is possible. This method will show you how to discover and then change those beliefs.

Step 1: Desire To Change

Step 2: Believe You Can Change

Step 3: Unlock Your Beliefs

Step 4: Design Your Reality

Step 1: You must WANT to change.

Making a permanent change must stem from a strong, inner desire to change. Real desire is not simply a whim or want; it is full of reasons, justifications, rationale and thoughts of how the change will benefit you and others when you make it. If you start making changes on a whim the changes won't last, take hold or create the results you want.

In my mid-twenties I dated a girl who was a smoker. She had been smoking for over five years by the time I met her and both her parents and older brother were smokers. Smoking is what was normal for her and a real part of her daily routines. I have never smoked and don't like being around smokers, but I fell in love with her and became tolerant of her smoking. She also made the compromise that she would only smoke outside the house and never in my car. One day she even made the ultimate compromise and decided to stop smoking altogether.

The way she went about quitting smoking was fascinating to me: she chose acupuncture. I had never tried acupuncture and didn't know anything about it, but she heard of a practitioner who claimed he could cure smoking and she was curious to try it. The treatment took just a few hours of her time and she came out of the session with a physical distaste and disgust for smoking. What the treatment had done was cause her to hate the taste and feeling of inhaling cigarette smoke. Unfortunately, what the acupuncture didn't do is change any of her patterns and habits.

After she left the acupuncturist's office, out of routine she reached for a cigarette and lit it up. She took one puff and immediately felt like throwing up. She couldn't even take a second puff and put out the cigarette. Over the course of the next few weeks, while I enjoyed her new smoke-free world, she continually fell back to her habits of picking up cigarettes and lighting them up. Each time she was disgusted by the taste and could only take one or two drags off each cigarette. Her smoking habits had still not changed and she wasn't even trying to change them. After another week she told me she couldn't stand it anymore and forced herself to smoke cigarettes until she overcame the acupuncturist's effects and got rid of the awful taste, replacing it with the satisfaction she had always received from the cigarettes. In a way, she proves that you can change if you truly want to; only she went in the opposite direction with her change.

I appreciated that she tried to quit smoking. But unfortunately, by only changing the surface of the problem (i.e. changing the physical result of smoking) and not addressing the behavior and reasons for smoking her willpower was actually turned against her desire to quit smoking. Her desire to NOT quit smoking overcame her desire to stop smoking, and she continued to smoke.

Change must start with a real desire to change, a desire that has the foundation of reason and rationale for all aspects of the change, not just the surface results. The Step 1 chapter discusses the desire to change in more detail and shows you how to create the intense desire necessary for success: a motivational desire.

Step 2: You must BELIEVE you can change.

You probably hear lots of people saying they can't be what they want to be (more successful, thinner, happier, etc). People who don't believe they can change will tell you all the reasons why they can't do something… "I could never be as thin as her because she's naturally skinny" … "I'll never make as much money as that guy because his father owns the company" … "I can't switch jobs because I'll never find the job I want". These types of phrases are negative and limiting, reinforcing the negative belief that you can't be who you want to be, and keeping you from changing.

Change requires you to believe you can make the change. You don't have to believe that you'll be the next Rockefeller to start making more money, but you do have to believe you can change yourself to achieve the goal of making more money.

One of the reactions I get from people when I tell them that I paid my way through the University of Southern California (an expensive, private university) is that they could never do what I did, or worse, they don't believe their child could go through what I went through. Although it was challenging, I loved my college experience. I worked 25 to 35 hours per week at different jobs off campus while taking a full schedule at school while maintaining good grades. There were many times during college when I woke up on a Monday morning with only $5 to my name and had to figure out how to eat and pay for gas until I got paid on Friday. Most people don't believe that they can work that hard and struggle that much… and as long as they believe that, they're right.

Financially, I survived college on one simple belief: if I needed the money, it would be there. Anyone could do what I did with that one belief because it led me to sources of money when I needed it. For example, on several occasions I started the week with only five dollars to my name. To get money for gas and food, I discovered that I could paid to give an opinion on a product in a marketing focus group – that was a quick $10, tripling the amount of money I could use during the week.

If you believe you can do something, then your brain will find a way to do it. Before you can truly make a change, you have to believe you can make the change. To make change simple for myself, I choose to believe that I can do anything I set my mind to, which includes changing my beliefs. The Step 2 chapter discusses beliefs and how to believe you can change in far greater detail.

NOTE: *The reason this is step two and not step one is because a desire can actually help you create a belief; if you had to create a belief before the desire, it would be more difficult to find the motivation to change.*

Step 3: Discover all the beliefs driving your behavior.

Step 3 is the fun part of making changes and I strongly suggest you write your thoughts down during this process. This step involves asking yourself questions in order to discover the beliefs that drive who you are. The brain is a powerful tool that will always give you an answer when you ask it a question. The trick is to give it a question that you want answered and in a way that will give you constructive answers. When it comes to the behavior you want to change, you need to ask yourself a few key questions:

1. What causes you to behave the way you do?
2. How do you feel when you behave in that way?
3. Who does your behavior affect?
4. When do you behave in the way you do?
5. Where or in what circumstances do you behave in that way?

The one question to be careful about asking is any question that starts with "why". As I said, your brain will always answer your question, but "why" questions often result in answers that aren't helpful or constructive. For example, if you are trying to lose weight and ask yourself "why do I always overeat at dinner?" you're likely to get negative answers like "because I can't control myself" or "because I'm an adult and can eat as much as I want". "Why" questions often result in self-defeating answers that rationalize the behavior versus help you understand it. Try to avoid these types of questions.

The answers to any of your questions might surprise you. Keeping with the losing weight questions above, if you were to ask yourself "what causes me to overeat at dinner" you might come up with several answers like:

- I love the taste of the food
- It's just a habit
- I grew up poor and eating a lot is a luxury
- I eat so fast I don't realize I'm full until it is too late

The great thing about answers like this is that you can take any and all of them and question these answers further. For example, "what causes me to eat so fast?". As you answer the new questions and build additional answers, keep asking questions of each answer.

The goal in this step is to begin uncovering the underlying reasons and beliefs that cause the current behavior. The closer you can get to the root cause of your behavior and beliefs, the more powerful and easy your change will become – it's like going back in time and making one decision differently that affects the rest of your life. With these questions and answers in mind, you'll repeat this step until you get down to the root cause of your behavior.

Keep asking yourself questions until you find the root cause for the behavior.

Repeating this step will help you trace back as far as possible to the root cause(s), and ultimately the core belief driving your current behavior. It is absolutely essential that you spend the time working through the questions and answers about yourself. Only you can answer the questions, which is why you are the only person who can change you. **You never have to share your answers with anyone else, so be bold, honest and direct with yourself.** If you believe that you overeat because you were poor and had to take what you got, go further. You might discover that you are still upset about being poor and that feeling is causing multiple other behaviors. Ask questions about how being poor made you feel and what caused you to be poor. As you progress and dig deeper you may discover that being poor is not the root cause and has nothing to do with why you overeat, but is the simple explanation you've been giving yourself to support a habit you don't want.

As you'll see in the next step, if you can change the root cause, then your current explanation and justification of your behavior will cease to exist, allowing you to easily change the behavior.

As a child, my family was relatively poor, living on welfare at one point in my childhood and always watching what we spent. When it came to food, we didn't eat a lot of expensive foods (for reasons of both cost and health), meaning we didn't get to have sodas, chips, cookies and other packaged foods. But when I got to stay with my aunt and uncle during the summer, they would spoil us with all sorts of things we wanted, like chips.

I remember my uncle handing me a large bag of nacho cheese flavored chips that was almost empty with just the broken pieces at the bottom of the bag. He told me to take it out to the garbage because he just opened a whole new bag. Since I had been poor all my young life, I could not understand why he would throw away perfectly good crumbs and argued with him. He again directed me to throw them away and I complied… almost. When I got to the dumpster, I decided to stuff both of my sweatshirt pockets full of as many chips as I could fit so at least I wasn't wasting what I could eat.

I came back into the house and began helping my uncle with whatever else he needed help with. Everything was going great until he caught me reaching into my pocket and pulling out chips! Fortunately, he wasn't angry and thought it was funny, but he did sit me down and explained to me that we had more chips and I didn't have to eat the leftover crumbs of the other bag. To this day I don't like to throw out food, but my reaction is no longer based on the behavior of being on welfare and being poor. I have changed my beliefs to ensure that I don't feel guilt that is based on something I couldn't control in my past, not my present. Now if I throw out food, my reasons are positive and not reactive or potentially negative.

Step 4: Choose new beliefs that will create the desired behavior.

Once you have identified the root cause of a behavior, you can choose to change how you feel about it. Change really is as simple as looking at one decision you made and choosing how you want that decision to affect you. While you can't change a decision that was made a long time ago, you CAN change your perspective on that decision, and therefore affect how you feel about that decision today. Changing how you feel about the root cause results in changing a core belief.

Changing your belief, feeling and emotion about some decision in your past will result in a trickle-effect through all the other decisions that lead to your current behavior. Many of our current behaviors can actually be traced back to teenage and adolescent years, though the older you are the more likely some of your decisions could have started later in life. Our challenges, failures and lessons in life shape everything we do and who we are. If those events happened when we were very young then they were probably out of our control.

For example, being poor during my childhood had many distinct effects on who I am and how I progressed in life. I remember the day I decided that I wanted to have a Mercedes when I grew up. One day when I was five years old, my mom took us to a Laundromat and a woman drove up in a grey Mercedes to go into an adjacent store. At the time I knew it was a nice car and that the woman had lots of money because she had something we couldn't afford, nor were allowed to have: a can of soda.

Recognizing that owning a Mercedes meant you were wealthy was a pivotal moment for my young mind. From that point forward I started looking at cars, money, wealth and what I thought it meant. I vowed at age five that I would not be poor when I grew up.

Looking back, my conclusions about money were rarely correct, nor entirely healthy. In fact, by age 13 I had decided and began telling everyone that I was going to be a millionaire by age 23. By age 20 my mom was fed up with hearing me talk about being a millionaire. Lucky for me she was able to articulate that having money was fine, but she was worried about my happiness and how I would react if I turned 23 and was not a millionaire. Her conversation spurred me to assess what caused my incessant behavior and talk about money and I looked all the way back to the woman driving the Mercedes.

When I looked back at my childhood and found the root cause of my behavior and discovered something as innocent as wanting to be wealthy enough to afford a soda, my entire adult perspective on money began to change. The irony about root causes is that when they're formed we often have no idea of what we really want. By the time I was 10 years old, we had plenty of money and could afford nice things (including soda, although my mom still wouldn't buy it for us), so the problem I identified at age five should have been solved, right? Wrong. It wasn't solved because I didn't know the belief needed to be changed. It was only resolved later as an adult when I found the root cause and chose to change how I felt about it.

Once you identify the root cause of your behavior, changing it merely requires you to decide how you want to feel about that cause. Because the root cause is usually so far in the past, it is easy to see why you felt the way you did at the time and why it's no longer necessary to feel that way now. In my case, I had no control over being poor so as an adult I decided that it simply didn't make sense to be unhappy about that aspect of my childhood. I also, by age 20, had drank enough sodas to make up for whatever I thought I missed out on as a child, and I can think of plenty of people who were far worse off than I was.

When you assess who you are and how you became who you are, you can easily see that your original feeling about a decision can be forgiven, forgotten, released and changed to something that benefits you now. How you feel about your life, yourself and decisions that affected you is completely your choice. Nobody can tell you how to feel about it, and in some cases you might not want to change how you feel about the root cause because that feeling has empowered other areas of your life you don't want to change.

Keep choosing to change each reason leading from the root cause.

After you identify the root cause and choose to change it (or not), look forward through your answers leading from the root cause back up to your current behavior. Like climbing up a tree to the outer branch where your behavior resides, you can now choose how you feel about yourself at each step of the way. As you assess your feelings about each answer and reason, you may find that the next answer becomes irrelevant and is already answered by the change you made at the root cause. In many cases you will make sufficient changes to your core beliefs and feelings that by the time you review the actual behavior you're trying to change you'll find that the behavior will be ridiculous, unnecessary and perhaps already changed.

Choose the behavior you desire and practice it.

I don't want to suggest that making changes to all your root causes will simply eliminate current behaviors, though it can in some cases depending on the complexity of the behavior. **What this methodology does for you is remove all the limiting beliefs**, the roadblocks and drivers of the behavior, so you can focus on changing the habitual nature of the behavior.

If my ex-girlfriend had figured out (hypothetically speaking) that the reason she smoked was because she wanted to be like her father and if she changed that belief she probably could have quit smoking much more easily. The acupuncture would have been very successful and she would have only had to deal with changing the habit of actually reaching for the cigarette in certain circumstances. But since she had not addressed the root cause, she was virtually powerless against the habit and quickly resumed smoking, overcoming the distaste and disgust she felt towards the cigarette.

Reprogramming your brain or changing yourself can be done in four steps: wanting to change, believing you can change, figuring out what to change, and making the change. Changes definitely take time and this process will get easier with practice and experience. To get started, all you have to do is identify something you want to change. Once you start making changes, you'll get more than just the reward of making the change. You'll also enjoy greater self-awareness and the power to look at your actions and decide to change them with ease. By the end of this book, you'll have all the tools you need to completely change who you are and become the person you deserve to be.

Chapter 2

Live life the way it COULD be, not the way it is

Step 1: Desire To Change

One of my favorite ways to test myself to see what I really want is when ordering food in a restaurant. I often see three or more entrees that all sound equally great and I can't decide which one I want. So I challenge myself to let my subconscious make the choice. I say to myself, "I'll just start ordering and whatever comes out of my mouth is obviously what I want". When the waiter asks for my order I'm always amazed at what happens: I place my order without hesitation. Instantaneously I go from a state of being completely undecided to a state of absolute decision. Sometimes I end up ordering what I think I'm going to order. Other times I order the meal that I was least sure about. In some rare instances, I'll even order something that wasn't even part of my three choices.

While ordering outside of my conscious choices seems strange enough to me, what's even more bizarre is when I don't challenge myself because I instantly see what I want and make up my mind. Then, when I place my I order, I suddenly find myself ordering something completely different! What is happening is that I have learned to trust my gut and allow my true desires to come forth. When the order is placed and I sit there stunned (and thankfully nobody notices), I realize that what I ordered really is what I wanted regardless of how decisive I started out.

The Power Of Desire

Desire is the second-most powerful motivator behind the pain of need. Obviously, if you have a real need, like air, food or water, then your drive will be incredibly strong and in many cases beyond your capability to ignore or hold back. Desire, like need, is a strong force that can drive many actions and comes in many intensities, some much stronger than others.

If you were to assemble all your desires together, it might resemble a community of people in a city where you're the mayor. As mayor you ultimately get to decide how, when and where to spend the city's money, but you'll have to contend with a bunch of different people vying for your attention and trying to persuade you. In real life, you're constantly faced with decisions that are balanced between your competing desires and needs. For example, if you received an unexpected $2,000 bonus at work and could spend it on anything you want, how would you spend it? How you would spend it is driven by your strongest desire – fix the air conditioning in the winter so you're ready for next summer or buy that new home theater system you want? The strength of your desires completely depends on your experiences and perspectives. If one of your children suffered heat stroke last summer because the A/C didn't work, you're much more likely to spend the money fixing the A/C and probably wouldn't give the entertainment system a moment's thought.

Changing yourself is most effective when you need to change, but how often are we **required** to change something about ourselves under threat of dire penalties? If you were diagnosed with allergies to milk and the result of having milk was itchy skin would that be enough pain to stop you from eating ice cream? What if milk, cheese and ice cream were part of your daily and weekly diet? Of course itchy skin, as a pain motivator, is pretty powerful, but it might not stop your habits because you may justify a certain amount of pain in order to continue eating ice cream.

On the other hand, if you want to change your eating habits related to dairy, you could if your desire was strong enough. To succeed in changing you must find your strongest desire to change. That type of desire is what I call a "motivational desire".

How To Create A Motivational Desire

This may seem self-evident to most, but it's worth stating: motivational desire stems from strong emotions like pain, love, fear, happiness, and can be supported by logic and reasoning when the results are painfully obvious. If you're contemplating a change you might only succeed if you draw strength from a motivational desire within you. It's a fact that most of us are 'ok' with our status quo but wish we could take that next step out of our rut. Until something drastic smacks us in the head we are more likely to continue our behavior of just being 'ok' than to even try to change it on our own.

Why wait until you have to change before you actually do? You can choose to change at any time – it's within your power if you have the desire. One of the ways in which people find their desire is by simply choosing a date to start their change. Of course, the further away that day is, the less likely the person is to succeed. Realistically, just setting a date to change is proof that you don't really want to change or, as we'll address later, don't believe you can change. When you find your motivational desire to change you'll be so driven to change that you won't be able to wait for that future date to arrive.

One of my favorite times of year is around the New Year because everyone is making their New Year's Resolutions. Honestly, I love any time that someone chooses to change, but I find it ironic that people anchor their desire to change on January 1st. New Year's Day is technically just like any other day of the year – you wake up, you eat, you do your thing and then you go to sleep and start over. Actually, New Year's Day is not like any other day because people sleep in, watch football, eat bad food and put off starting their resolutions until January 2nd. Why not just start your new behavior now instead of waiting until January 1 or 2? Really, it doesn't matter and I am truly excited by people who decide to change and embark on their journey towards that goal. But if we can realize that the power of New Year's Day is rooted within the value we place on that day, the symbolism of a new beginning, then we can realize the ability to empower ourselves with the same vigor on any other day of the year too.

Empowering ourselves with a desire that is strong enough to facilitate our change is what it takes to create a motivational desire. Anything less will easily fade and cave in to competing desires.

To create a motivational desire, start by weighing the benefits and consequences of the behavior you want to change. As we'll discuss later in this chapter, sometimes we already have reasons for change and they are sufficient to carry us through the process. Even in those cases it helps to make sure those reasons are as strong as possible by reviewing the benefits and consequences.

EXERCISE (Part 1): Weigh The Benefits

It is often difficult to figure out why you should change by your thoughts alone. To make it easier, try this exercise of weighing the benefits and the consequences of changing vs. not changing. You'll be able to write down your results and more easily see a way to develop your motivational desire for change.

1. On a piece of paper (or on your computer) draw a large "T" where you can write down some answers to the questions below (see example below).
2. At the top of one column, write down "Keep" and on the other write "Change".

KEEP	CHANGE

You will now use this t-bar graph to write down your answers to the following, opposing questions:

Keep The Behavior	Change The Behavior
What benefit do I get from my behavior?	What benefit would I get from changing?
Who benefits from my behavior?	Who benefits when I change?

3. In the ***KEEP*** column write down the reasons why you should **keep** the behavior and in the ***CHANGE*** column write down your reasons to **change** the behavior (see example below). At this point, you can look for the factors that are the most powerful in your mind. If the most powerful factor is on the side of keeping the behavior, then you've identified one of the key factors that will make changing difficult.

KEEP	CHANGE
I'm comfortable.	I could feel happier.
I won't have to spend money.	Life would be easier.
Nobody benefits.	

4. Next, if you don't already see a decisive reason to change or stay the same, then weight each reason and assign a value from 1 to 100, with 100 being the strongest. You can assign any number of points you want as the weighting is simply meant to display how strongly you feel about each reason.

5. After assigning the values count the total weight of all the factors from both sides and see which side is higher.

	KEEP		CHANGE
50	I'm comfortable.	60	I could feel happier.
80	I won't have to spend money.	70	Life would be easier.
0	Nobody benefits.		
130	TOTAL	130	TOTAL

After you have weighted your answers, continue on to the next section. Don't worry if your results are still equally weighted and there isn't an obvious choice yet. These results help you see which answers and reasons are going to be the most challenging or easiest for you to handle during your change.

EXERCISE (Part 2): Weigh The Consequences

The next step is to look at the consequences of your behavior by answering these questions:

Keep The Behavior	Change The Behavior
Who will my behavior affect in the long-run?	If I change my behavior, who will I affect and how?
What will happen if I stay the same?	What will happen if I change?

I Can Change If I Want To

Just like you did for the benefits, list out the consequences for staying the same and the consequences for changing. If the benefits alone don't give you a clear indication, putting the consequences into the same context as the benefits will help you build your case. Identify the most powerful consequence you listed and compare it to the most powerful benefit. Or, assign a weight to each consequence (1 to 100, with 100 being the most powerful) and add up the totals for each side.

The table below completes the example by showing the weighted consequences along with the benefits. As may be the case for you, when you add in the value of the consequences, even if the benefits are equal, you may find a huge difference between why you should change or stay the same. Ultimately, seeing these weighted values can help you form a motivational desire to make the change.

KEEP		CHANGE	
Benefits			
50	I'm comfortable.	60	I could feel happier.
80	I won't have to spend money.	70	Life would be easier.
0	Nobody benefits.		
130	TOTAL	130	TOTAL
Consequences			
0	I will be affected.	50	I will be affected.
0		75	I could attract better people.
0		100	I will achieve my goals
0	TOTAL	225	TOTAL
130	GRAND TOTAL	355	GRAND TOTAL

If the results of this exercise still haven't helped you see a clear reason to change, then it is possible that changing simply isn't worthwhile for you. It is possible that what you think you should change or want to change really isn't the right focus and perhaps there is some other facet of yourself you should be looking at. Then again, maybe you just didn't give yourself real answers or all the answers to each of the questions above, so dig deeper and come up with more reasons.

Once you're done with this exercise and you have sufficient reasons why you should change, then you can start to use these supporting answers to create your motivational desire. I say 'start' because you need to bolster the strength of this desire even further.

Measure Your Past

The next step is to measure how your behavior matches up to the benefits and consequences you just assessed. Review all the times you can think of when you exhibited your current behavior and see if there is a pattern and/or additional factors. What you will probably find is a list of supporting examples for why you should change.

For example, if you like drinking socially but all your friends tell you that you are a mean drunk, you might want to change that behavior and become a happy drunk. Perhaps you discovered by asking the questions above that the last time you were drunk you hurt a good friend with your actions. The pain of hurting that friend might be strong enough alone to cause you to change. To be sure it is strong enough it helps to look at your behavior in other situations too. As you look back over the times you drank a lot you might see a pattern of negative consequences like losing friends, losing belongings, causing damage to property, getting into fights, etc. Each of these past experiences adds to the reasons why you should change by helping you realize that, over time, your behavior has a sufficiently high cost.

An Example Of Changing An Emotional Reaction

When I fell in love for the first time, I was suddenly struck with new emotions and feelings I had never truly experienced. From an intellectual perspective, I could see what the emotions might mean and I thought I would never experience some of the more negative emotions like jealousy. In fact, I found myself to be jealous quite often. If I saw my girlfriend give anyone other than a family member a hug, I would immediately become jealous. It was not as though she was doing anything unnatural or immoral that should solicit my reaction, I was just reacting with jealousy for some unknown reason.

The most important aspect of feeling jealous was how I felt as a result. I didn't like myself. I became cold, angry, hurt and distant. She felt it too. My reactions caused her to react in kind, at first being sympathetic to my feelings, and then playful, and then resentful and it went downhill from there. It was easy for me to see that this one emotion, jealousy, was causing me to not feel love and I was losing my relationship. Luckily, I realized that I didn't necessarily have to feel that way, nor did I have to let this aspect of myself cause a wonderful relationship to spiral negatively out of control.

Obviously, I recognized that I could make a change to not feel jealous. Using this methodology, I set out to change myself, and the first step was to create a motivational desire. My answers to the questions above are shown in the table on the next page with their respective weightings.

KEEP		CHANGE	
What Are Benefits From Behavior		*What Are Benefits From Changing*	
50	Jealousy keeps me alert to potential trouble or risk of my girlfriend straying away.	35	I could feel happy about seeing my girlfriend even if she just hugged another guy (she is with me, after all, and not him)
20	Being jealous helps me build strength to confront someone trying to hit on my girlfriend	50	I wouldn't have difficult arguments to go through
5	Jealousy creates tension in the relationship and causes my girlfriend to come to me.	35	I wouldn't feel negative emotions over something trivial and harmless
		60	I wouldn't ruin anyone's day by being upset or angry
		90	I could keep a good relationship instead of losing it
Who Benefits From Behavior		*Who Benefits From Changing*	
20	I benefit when the emotion of jealousy is warranted	50	I do
		50	My girlfriend
		25	My friends who are around both my girlfriend and I (because there is no unnecessary drama)
95	**TOTAL**	**395**	**TOTAL**
Consequence Of Staying The Same		*Consequences Of Changing*	
0	I will always be affected by the behavior	50	I will be affected
0	Any girl I have a relationship with could be affected	50	Any girl I have a relationship would be affected
0	My family and friends could all be affected	25	My family and friends would be saved from being affected negatively
What Will Happen If I Stay The Same		What Will Happen If I Change	
0	My relationships will continue to have difficult times whenever I see My girlfriend	50	It will be easier to be happy about seeing my girlfriend
		25	I can focus my energy on more

I Can Change If I Want To

	hug someone else		productive uses
0	I will become guarded and mistrustful of my future girlfriends	100	I won't feel trapped by an emotion that is triggered by trivial events
0	I will not feel free to love and be happy because I'm constantly struck with jealousy	25	I will be more free to love and treat someone better
0	I may never be successful in a relationship	50	My relationships are more likely to succeed
0	**TOTAL**	375	**TOTAL**
95	**GRAND TOTAL**	770	**GRAND TOTAL**

You can see by the total points I gave to each attribute that it is completely obvious that I should change (remember that the weighting was arbitrarily set by how I felt about each attribute). There is little reason to stay the same!

As I worked through these questions for myself, it became immediately obvious to me that being jealous and not changing the way I felt about jealousy was not going to work or help me be happy. It was apparent that I needed to change and I had a whole list of reasons why. Now not only did I have a desire to change I had supporting reasons on paper to help me continue to choose to change. Wanting to have a happy, successful relationship, backed by all the benefits and consequences, became my motivational desire to change. Plus, this list is something I could come back to for reinforcement and reminders of my desire to change if at any time I lost my motivation.

If your answers are not as clear, or you're sitting on the fence or even contemplating not changing, then it's time to get tough and look even deeper. Perhaps logic, reasoning or the answers you've provided for yourself are not strong enough. Maybe you should look at the pain of not changing, the pain of staying the same. Pain is the ultimate motivator, after all.

Pain Is The Ultimate Motivator

While a strong desire to change can root from many things, including pain, it would be nice if we didn't have to feel the pain and could just leave it out of the equation. However, in most cases our desires do come from some form of pain, whether physical, mental, emotional or even spiritual. As much as I hope you can find strength and energy to change for positive non-pain-filled reasons, you may have to look at the pain your behavior causes before you can truly find the desire to change.

My father is a substance abuse counselor, so I have seen a few examples of how pain can drive someone to change their addictions to alcohol and drugs. In fact, I have seen my father recover from being both a drug user and an alcoholic through the strength of the pain he realized as a result of his actions.

You may be thinking that addiction is too extreme of an example to show you how to change your more benign problems. Being addicted to a serious drug like cocaine seems like a far cry from being jealous, or being afraid of public speaking, or going out in public in a bathing suit. But is it really all that different? The results are the same: you can't change because you are held back by fears and limiting beliefs. Regardless of the gravity and seriousness of what you're trying to change, you still haven't found the motivational desire to change and realizing the pain of your actions may help you find that desire.

If drug use has caused you to lose your family, your job, your money, your friends, then it is easy to see the amount of pain that could be used as the motivation to get off drugs. The same can be said for any other change you want to make. If being afraid to stand in front of an audience has caused you to lose out on a job promotion, or an opportunity to interview for a better job, or to be the lead singer in a band, then the same pain of failure and continuing failure is pretty easy to see as a motivating factor. The challenge for you is to look at all these results and link them together to see the pain. Unfortunately, most of us, me included, have been caught looking the other direction instead of at the total consequences and results. It's just too easy to ignore the problem one more time.

I'm very fortunate that my father realized what his drug and alcohol use was doing to him, not to mention everyone around him. It only took him a few years to come to terms and then make the change and now he helps others win the battle. Another one of my friends was not as lucky and his "intervention", as he calls it, was in the back of an ambulance as he was being revived from death after a drug overdose. Fortunately, he survived and realized that he could not afford to stay the same.

Certainly, it is my hope that you don't need to suffer the penalty of nearly dying before you find your motivational desire to make the change. In fact, you can make the choice to simply stop reading right now and spend the next 15 minutes writing out the answers to the questions above. Taking action now will help you recognize the consequences and more easily identify the pain that is being caused now and/or in the future, which will lead to your motivational desire. Consider my own projection of not changing my jealous reactions – I honestly saw that I might never be successful in a relationship and constantly feel trapped by the pain of jealousy. The current pain plus impending pain was all I needed to drive my desire to change.

Even if pain is not enough of a reason to change, then there is still another way to find your motivation to change. It's the same manner in which you formed the current behavior: logic and justification.

Logical Reasons To Change

Have you ever heard yourself answer a question with a justifying reason that wasn't really honest or true to why you're doing something? I was told once that if you have to justify something you're doing, it's probably because you already know it's not the right thing to do. Fortunately for all of us, our brains are so powerful that it doesn't care whether we are justifying something positive or negative (if it did care, we wouldn't be able to justify harmful behaviors). What this means is that you can use logical reasons and justifications to undo your behavior just as well as you used them to create the behavior.

One of my friends was the perfect salesman. He was amazing when it came to gaining people's favors, earning their trust and helping them realize that they needed to purchase whatever he was selling. But the irony of his skills is that he constantly used them to sell himself and those around him on doing things that didn't always make sense, or things the rest of us wouldn't normally do. Not to pick on him too terribly, but does anyone really need a new cell phone every 3 to 6 months? In his case, he did. His reasons were:

- to keep up with technology (because he was in technology sales),
- to make his life more effective (though it rarely did),
- to create opportunities to converse with people (which usually did work!)

- and to show how innovative he was (which rarely, if ever, contributed to winning a sale).

I always loved the second reason because he would invite me, as his 'tech-guru', to help him set up this newest device that often wasn't even on the market yet. For me it meant that we had a reason to hang out and grab some food, plus I always enjoyed playing with the newest technology. But after awhile, it turned out he was attempting to satisfy much bigger needs than the ones he claimed. To my knowledge, he never was able to use the phone to actually become more efficient than the previous phone (hence, never achieving a return on investment) and this habit of buying new phones started showing up in other purchases (high-end watches, artwork, alcohol, clothing, etc).

While that's an example of the power of logic and justifications for creating and/or supporting a potentially negative behavior, you can just as easily use this exact same method to create a motivational desire to change to a good behavior. Simply start justifying the reasons you **should** change. For example, I could tell myself (and others) that NOT being jealous will make me happier and more fun to be around. Plus, with all the energy I would save, I could focus more on my work and become more successful. Even better, my girlfriend won't be able to justify getting upset if I hug a friend who happens to be a girl. Even my friends and family could benefit and like me more if I change!

None of my justifications may actually be true. The reality is that simply not being jealous may only eliminate one reason for being unhappy and not create a new reason to be happy. Or that 'saved energy' may never be utilized in any new ways and therefore I won't truly become more successful. But, as you'll read about in the next chapter, your brain doesn't care about reality it only cares about what you tell it to believe. Our minds are designed to create the outcomes that are based upon the information we feed ourselves. Feed yourself justifications to not change and you'll remain the same by reinforcing your position. Feed yourself justifications to change and you'll find the motivational desire to change.

Before you read the next chapter, ask yourself if you really want to change or not. The motivation to change has to be a strong, driving force that will help you win many battles that are yet to come. As you battle to change, you will be presented with entirely new ideas, perspectives and perceptions about why you shouldn't change. You may find trying to change is just like starting a new diet and struggling not to eat dessert. If your motivation is strong enough, you'll win the dessert battle every time. But if your motivation isn't well grounded and you start to make contrary choices, your change won't take effect.

But don't worry... this method is not like your typical diet or a battle of wills. **All I'm asking you to do right now is confirm that you truly want to change by finding your motivational desire.** The next step (to believe you can change) is going to lay the groundwork for your path to success using your desire as the fuel. The reason this method requires you to want to change before believing you can change is to fuel your belief in yourself and in your own power to evolve. With all sincerity, the main reason we can't change isn't for a lack of desire, it's for a lack of belief. But if I asked you (or myself) to believe in something you don't want, it will be much harder to find the belief that will get us out of our ruts.

Now, with your motivational desire in hand, I'll show you how easy it really is to create and mold the beliefs you want.

Chapter 3

Confidence is knowledge of yourself

Step 2: Believe You Can Change

Before we go into detail about believing you can change, let's discuss beliefs and how to create them. While all you need in this step is to simply believe you are capable of changing, believing is easier said than done for most people. So how do you believe you can change? It helps to understand how beliefs work and impact your life, then to see how they are formed, including how you can form the beliefs you desire.

What You Believe Is Your Reality

I live my life by a simple phrase: "What you believe IS your reality". If you think about this phrase, not just dismiss it, but really think about it, you start to see that your beliefs form the reality you experience. I have been told by countless people that this phrase is just too simple. They write it off because it is so obvious (and aren't the best ideas always the simplest?) never really taking the time to understand that this one phrase is the key to how we view and interact with the world. It is the key to change. It is the key to your mind. **It is the key to changing your mind!**

What if you could change just one belief and suddenly become more successful? Or lose more weight? Or be happier? Or be a better parent? Or find the power to survive a difficult situation? You can if you understand that your beliefs literally form your reality. You can if you choose to believe that you control your reality and views through your beliefs. You can if you choose to believe that you can change your beliefs.

Reality is an interesting word that is highly misconstrued by most people because it can support multiple meanings. Webster's online dictionary defines reality as:

reality:

1. the state or quality of being real.

2. resemblance to what is real.

3. a real thing or fact.

4. real things, facts, or events taken as a whole; state of affairs: the reality of the business world; vacationing to escape reality.

5. Philosophy. a. something that exists independently of ideas concerning it. b. something that exists independently of all other things and from which all other things derive.

6. something that is real.

7. something that constitutes a real or actual thing, as distinguished from something that is merely apparent.

If Webster has so many ways to explain reality, then it's no wonder the definition of 'reality' can be misconstrued and interpreted by people in so many different ways. Which of these definitions do you find to be the most relevant to you? For our purposes, the context of the reality our beliefs form, the first definition is all we need: "the state or quality of being real".

For you and me, as humans, we deal with what is real and factual through our perceptions of reality. Here's an example: temperature. How is it possible that 55 degrees can feel cold to one person and warm to another?

If you've ever lived in a cold climate that receives snow during the winter, you know that your body becomes acclimated to cold temperatures. Not that you're ever truly comfortable in really cold weather, but when you spend a winter in below-freezing temperatures and the temperature suddenly rises over freezing, it feels warm outside to you. As a kid I lived in Salt Lake City, Utah where the winters are between 15 and 30 degrees Fahrenheit for months on end. When spring came and temperatures rose to 55 degrees, it felt warm enough to walk the mile to school wearing only shorts and a sweatshirt. As kids, we celebrated how warm it was outside.

On the other hand, if you've only lived in a warm climate, then 55 degrees feels like it's 'freezing' outside. Now that I have lived in Southern California for many years, I am quite comfortable with temperatures in the 70's and above. On those rare days that it is 55 degrees outside, I must wear pants, a sweater, a jacket and even gloves and a hat if I'm going to be outside for any length of time. Even now as I write, it is 70 degrees inside and 60 degrees outside and I'm wearing a long-sleeve shirt with a thick sweater over it.

Why is that? How can the temperature, an unchangeable fact, feel warm to one person and cold to another? I'm certain you will agree that how we feel about or perceive the temperature is relative to what we're accustomed to. You can even read stories about Antarctic expeditions where people become acclimated to negative 20 (F) degree weather and they start to sweat when the temperatures rise above positive 10 (F).

So why is this important? Because what you believe about a situation, whether what you believe is based on facts, experience, physical or mental conditions, creates your reality. If you lived in Antarctica, your reality would prove to you that 55 degrees is downright hot!

What I refer to as 'reality' in this book is your unique perceptions and experiences about facts. You can't change a fact – 55 degrees is 55 degrees no matter how you measure it. But you can change your perspective of what 55 degrees means to you, just as you can change your perspective of what any other fact means to you. The fact may be that my girlfriend hugged another guy. Does that fact require me to become jealous? Of course not. **How I feel about a fact is my reality based on my beliefs.** Hence, you can't change the facts, only your attitude.

Defining Reality Through Beliefs

I have another way to explain how beliefs form your reality. Let's draw a bulls-eye target with four circles. The innermost circle is reality, which is surrounded by your thoughts, which are encompassed by your beliefs, which are surrounded by facts.

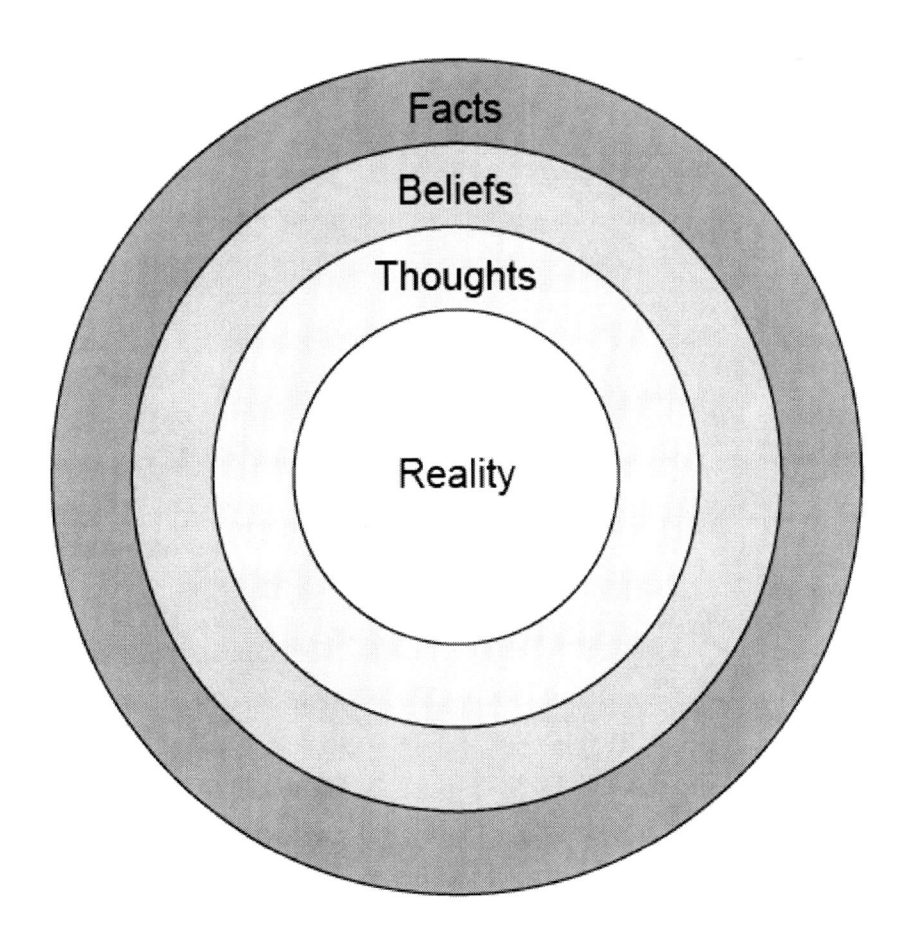

By definition:

- **Facts** are what is real without perception – they cannot be controlled.
- **Beliefs** are the rules you define to interpret and deal with facts.
- **Thought** is the process you use to interpret facts through your beliefs
- **Reality** is your perception of the world based on the process of interpreting facts through your beliefs.

In order to get to your reality, you have to start with the facts and work those facts through your belief system and thought processes before you see your reality. But isn't it easier to just start with reality and forget the rest? Reality is, after all, what we experience and what's right in front of us, right? Most of the time we see the world in the opposite order starting with our reality, which makes it very difficult to change ourselves.

By starting with reality and not the facts, we tend to only see foregone conclusions that we can't change, even treating those conclusions as though they are facts when they are not. If you wake up in the morning and know you have to exercise but can only see that it's cold, then your reality may tell you that it's too cold outside to go for your morning jog.

Focusing on your reality (it's too cold outside) has a pre-determined result (not jogging) and we all know you can't change the temperature outside, so you can't change reality either. Starting from the perspective of reality, which is the result of interpreting facts through your beliefs and thoughts, means that you see only the end result which by itself cannot be changed. What can be changed are your thoughts and your beliefs.

The reason for this bulls-eye chart is to help you reverse the way you look at yourself and your world so you can be empowered to change your beliefs which directly control your reality. When you work from the outside-in, moving towards the bulls-eye, you look at the facts first (not reality) and attempt to see what beliefs you use to interpret those facts. Reversing your view of reality allows you to see how your perspective or reality can actually be changed when you change your beliefs and thoughts.

Let's continue with the example that it is 55 degrees outside. If you **believe** that temperature to be cold (for any reason) then you can next look at how your thoughts behave as a result. Because you believe it's cold outside your thoughts may immediately process all the effects of being cold (pain, struggle, hassle, etc). Thinking that it's cold outside before you even step out the door is not a pleasant thought. Suddenly it becomes apparent why your reality about the temperature outside keeps you from deciding to go for that morning jog.

Now for the fun part. Let's start over, but this time we'll consider choosing a different belief and see what happens. Ok, so it's 55 degrees outside. What if you believed that to be warm? If you believed that 55 degrees was warm your thoughts would then behave in a way that supports you going for a jog. You might think, "wow, it's so nice to go running when it's warm outside because it's not so hot that I sweat too much – oh, I can't wait to get some fresh air". Your thoughts, based on you believing that it's warm outside, will reinforce the positive feelings you get from the opposite of being cold. As a result, your reality empowers you to achieve your goals of physical fitness, which has a domino-effect of feeling good about yourself, viewing the weather in a positive light and generally starting your day in the right direction. Next thing you know, based on this one little belief, you've become more friendly and happier, probably telling everyone you meet how warm it is.

To be fair, it may not be that easy to simply *believe* that 55 degrees is warm, but that's not the point. You could just as easily consider the belief that 55 degrees is the perfect temperature to go jogging because the cold air really jump-starts your energy level. **The point is to show you that WHAT you believe DEFINES your reality.** Everything you believe drives your thoughts and controls how you experience the world. Unfortunately for you pessimists out there who hate to hear this, I'm talking about whether we choose to see the glass half-empty or half-full. The fact is that half of the glass's volume contains a liquid. How you perceive that glass is entirely up to you and your beliefs.

An Example Of How Beliefs Create Reality

When I was in college I took a business communications class that taught us how to present to an audience. The majority of people in this world do not like public speaking, and it is ranked as one of the most stressful events – right up there with death, divorce, and other life-changing events. Fortunately for everyone in my class we were all in the same predicament: we were all equally afraid, we had to present to each other and we were being filmed so we could review our own presentation afterwards.

I've always known that I wanted to be able to speak to a large crowd and when I took that communications class and discovered how hard it was, I was suddenly challenged. How was I going to become a good public speaker if I was so scared of it? This was another time in my life when I looked at my reality and beliefs. With the motivational desire to become a public speaker already built into my long-term career goals, I looked for a way to reduce the fear and nervousness. When I started looking at the facts, I discovered a few interesting things about public speaking (thanks to my professor for pointing some of these things out).

1. As a public speaker, the audience is there to listen to you therefore YOU are the expert at that moment and are empowered to act like the expert.
2. Whether you're presenting to 1,000 people or only one person, you still have the same goal to impart the information you have to present.
3. The best public speakers are not nervous, they are comfortable and seem to enjoy being on stage.

As I looked at my beliefs about public speaking I discovered a few interesting things about how I viewed speaking. I believed that:

1. If I messed something up I would lose people's trust
2. If I got nervous, I might pass out or get sick
3. If I didn't become good at public speaking, I would fail in business
4. If I wasn't a good speaker I was a failure

Then, as I reviewed my thoughts around these beliefs, I uncovered a critical thought process that framed my reality: I didn't LIKE public speaking. If you look at each of my beliefs, they are all negative and my thoughts naturally wrapped negative thoughts around those beliefs and resulted in my not liking being a presenter. Then it struck me: how can I become good at something I don't like to do?

As you go through your own process of looking at your thoughts and beliefs related to a fact, if you come to a question like I did, a question that contradicts what you're trying to do, answer it!

How can I become good at something I don't like to do? The answer is that I can't. So then I asked myself more questions. My first question was a challenge to my motivational desire: do I really want to become a good speaker? The answer was yes. My next question was: if I did like public speaking could I become good at it? The answer was yes. Then the most important question came to me… could I enjoy public speaking? The answer was yes! Was there any reason I couldn't learn to actually enjoy public speaking? Not really, especially if I looked at my beliefs and challenged them to support my desire to enjoy speaking.

In the coming pages we'll talk in more detail about how to create or change beliefs, but to finish this example, I'll summarize what I did to change my reality about public speaking. The first thing I did was choose to believe that I LOVED public speaking. I looked at each of my negative beliefs and found ways to dismiss them, explain them away or ignore them entirely.

If I love public speaking then:

1. My desire to be the best speaker would help me recover from messing up and losing people's trust, and work harder to reduce the risk of messing up in the future.

2. I can find ways to reduce my nervousness before, during and after the speaking event.

3. I will succeed at business regardless of whether I am good at speaking or not.

4. I can accept that I may fail as a speaker at least some of the time and each failure is a new opportunity to learn and grow.

The result of believing that I loved public speaking was that my thoughts became positive, supportive and encouraging. As I began changing my beliefs through my college semester, I became more and more enthusiastic and excited about speaking and even started seeking opportunities to speak outside class. The greatest result is that I have achieved my dream of presenting to large crowds without notes or speaking aides. Although I didn't at first, today I truly do enjoy public speaking. Today I enjoy the reality I formed by changing my beliefs.

The World Is Full Of Options

I am an optimist and while I believe everybody could benefit from some optimism, I also value multiple perspectives. I often need people who represent other perceptions of the world on my side, not just the optimists. I need a good pessimist, pragmatist and realist to help me balance my views and actions to ensure I make good decisions throughout life. We all need a balance in how we approach the world or our species would take too many risks and quickly become extinct.

This concept of what you believe is your reality is not meant to turn you into a zealot that overly emphasizes the possibilities rather it is a way to help you see that you can control your view of the world by controlling what you believe. I believe that the world is full of options and every decision we make is comprised of 43 different paths. Why 43?!? Well why not? 43 is a nice arbitrary number that's big enough to remind us that there are more paths than we typically see at first glance. It is the companion concept to "what you believe is your reality" because each path shows you how a different choice (or belief) affects your outcome.

What if you woke up on Monday with only $5 to your name, what would you do? What are your choices? If you know that you have to pay your rent on Friday and that you won't get paid enough by Friday to cover the costs, how will you do it? This is where recognizing your choices can help you form or expand your reality to feel the way you want to feel about a fact (e.g. the fact that you don't have enough money to pay rent).

Here are just some of the possible paths to consider for how you're going to pay your rent.

1. Earn more money.
2. Sell something you own.
3. Borrow money.
4. Pay late.
5. Steal money.
6. Move out of your apartment.
7. Win the lottery.
8. Get a roommate.
9. Negotiate a lower rent payment.
10. Barter with your landlord.
11. Come up with a sympathy-inducing excuse (like your mother just died and you have to pay for the funeral)
12. Go out of town until Monday.

These are only a dozen random options and I'm sure you can think of many more if you try. Did you notice option # 5 – steal money? Do you agree with that option? From a moral perspective, I hope not. But really, isn't that an option just like any other method to get money? When I was poor in college I never stole money, but it helped to consider all the possible choices and then to choose the one I liked the best or that met my needs the best.

Looking at your options helps you see that there are other beliefs you can choose in relation to a fact. Just as you have many different choices for how you make a decision, you have many different beliefs to choose from in how you decide what your reality is. By choosing to see the world as a set of many choices you also open yourself up to seeing multiple ways of believing and ultimately achieving your goal to change.

Recognizing your options creates an interesting side-effect: *you get to know yourself better.*

Most people would never even consider stealing money to pay their rent as an option because they already know they don't steal. But have you ever thought through the reasons why you wouldn't steal in order to pay the rent? You're certainly not going to go out and steal money simply because it is an option, so don't be afraid to consider it as a real option. What you get by recognizing and thinking through the outcome of a negative option is the power to make a conscious choice about a belief. When you have actually thought through the reason(s) why you won't steal, you are that much more aware of who you are inside and what you believe.

Understanding your beliefs through viewing your life as a set of choices and a set of beliefs is the basis for how you perceive and experience reality, which leads us to how we can change or create a belief to achieve the change we want.

How To Create A Belief

I don't know about you, but nobody ever sat me down as a kid and told me how to create a belief. Beliefs just sort of happened. They form through the influence of those we trust and look up to. They form through the results of our experiences. They also form through the repetition of thought, like a stream carving out a canyon over time. They form as the result of trauma and achievement. Or, more concisely stated, **beliefs are formed by the thoughts you give the most value to as they enter and are processed by your brain.**

In traumatic experiences the strength of your emotional thoughts during the event can instantly form or change your beliefs. Take, for example, what you would believe about the risks of wearing a seatbelt while driving as a teenager when you have no experience with cars vs. after you've had an accident without (or even with) a seatbelt. When you have a car accident, your beliefs about seatbelts, among other things, are instantly formed and solidified because of the weight or value you associate with the consequences of the accident. If the seatbelt saved your life, you'll never go without one again. If you didn't have a seatbelt on and went to the hospital, you'll probably always wear them going forward. On the other hand, if not wearing a seatbelt was the only thing that saved your life, you may believe that seatbelts are the wrong device to rely upon for your safety.

During my senior year in high school when I got my license I was racing around on a local mountain road when I came around a corner really fast. It was a blind corner and just as I came around it I saw a guy and girl in the middle of the road with their truck flipped over. I barely stopped in time to avoid hitting them – their accident had just happened and I was first on the scene. Their truck was totaled, their belongings strewn across the road and, remarkably, neither of them hurt. The reason I recount this story is because these two people were in the same accident but had completely different stories of the event. The guy who sat in the passenger seat was excitedly telling me that he rode out the roll-over with the SUV because he was buckled in and he barely had a scratch. Then the girl, who had been driving, told me she was thrown from the vehicle and landed in the middle of the road on her butt (showing me the scrape she got). I was confused. How did she get thrown from the car? Turns out she hadn't clicked in her seat belt yet and her driver side window was open so as the truck flipped she was ejected out her door window. The scary thing is that the door and roof on her side was crushed in from the truck landing on that side. Had she been buckled in she would have been in the hospital or worse. Imagine being so lucky! Now try to imagine what each of them believes about seatbelts.

Fortunately, you don't need to have a car accident to learn how to create or change a belief. One of the aspects of growing up and maturing is realizing you can form your own beliefs; you don't have to accept the beliefs you grew up with. No matter what age any of us grow to, we can always choose a new belief if we have the desire to.

Creating A Belief

Given that beliefs are the rules we define to interpret and deal with facts, then creating a belief is as plain as defining a new rule in relation to a fact. What rules you define are completely up to you and within your control. Most of the beliefs we have are formed naturally and without our conscious effort and involvement. Rarely does someone say to themselves, "I'm going to create a new belief today" and then do it. Using the method in this book can certainly make that concept possible, but forming beliefs does not have to be an activity we schedule as a task. Rather, I suggest you look at creating a belief in the same way that water sculpts canyons – it is shaped over time through repetition.

In other words, you have to work on creating and reinforcing the belief until it becomes part of who you are. As I said earlier, beliefs are formed by the thoughts you give the most value as they enter your brain and continue to circulate in your thoughts. The simplest concept to creating a belief, then, is to repetitively think the same thought and assign the thought a high value by working it into your way of thinking.

To make the process more clear, here are several methods for forming beliefs through your thought process:

- repeat the new belief like a mantra
- each time the old belief enters your thoughts repeat your new belief eight times
- think about the belief during certain daily events (e.g. eating, going to sleep, etc)
- tell others about your new belief
- read articles and books that support your new belief
- discuss the new belief with others
- practice the new belief
- reward yourself for employing the belief
- punish yourself for not employing the belief (if you respond better to negative reinforcement)

Any method, including the examples above, that causes your new belief to work its way into your thought processes will help it solidify and take root. Forming a belief is no different than forming a habit, except that most of us are blind to the habits we start. Did you know it takes 21 days to form or break a habit? Forming a belief doesn't have to take that long, but it can, depending on how often you put the belief into your thoughts.

To fully solidify your new belief, there's one more thing you should do: reinforce it with examples. Thinking a belief won't always make it true, especially if you counteract the thoughts with competing beliefs, nor will your brain be likely to accept the belief without proof. You need to show yourself examples of why you believe these new thoughts – this is where your motivational desire comes in and where you need to value your thoughts.

When you read about creating a motivational desire, I showed you how to weigh the benefits and consequences of what you want to change. If you chose to change, you should have found that the benefits and consequences TO change far outweighed the benefits and consequences of not changing. This weight helped you reinforce your desire. This same weight is exactly the kind of value you need to assign to your new belief.

I'll go back to the example of changing myself to no longer feel jealousy. Step one was to find the motivational desire to change, which I found and demonstrated in my example. Step two is to believe I can change to no longer feel jealousy. By itself, the belief that I don't have to feel jealous is difficult to believe because my emotional reaction to events will completely counteract the new belief. But if I spend time reviewing all the benefits and consequences TO change, and relate those reinforcing values with the thought "I do not get jealous", I will give my belief weight and value in my mind. For example, instead of just telling myself to not feel jealous, I would tell myself "I do not get jealous because" and insert one of the reasons to change (e.g. "I do not get jealous because I want to be successful in relationships", "I do not get jealous because I refuse to feel trapped by that emotion", "I do not get jealous because I do not want to get upset or angry", etc.). All these reinforcements of the belief that I don't have to be jealous really translate into believing that I can change.

As an example of how beliefs are formed, have you ever been told something by someone that you instantly thought was true? Someone told me that all pomegranates (a fruit that contains individual juicy seeds) contained the exact same number of seeds and that number corresponds with a religious book in some manner. The fact is that pomegranates produce varying number of seeds depending on their size and there is zero correlation between the number of seeds and a religious text. But the so-called fact was so intriguing my friend thought it to be true. Since she thought it was intriguing, she started telling others the same bad information. The more she told it, the more she believed it, never questioning its validity and all too happy to keep telling others. I probably shouldn't have done it, but I'm a bit skeptical of "facts" like that, so I did a little research and found an article disproving it. When I showed my friend the article, she actually disputed the article and defiantly stuck to her belief. I have no idea what reasons she had to continue believing the falsehood, but her belief was so strong even factual proof couldn't change her belief.

Your belief system can be complicated. My friend's belief about the pomegranate seeds probably formed because she heard the information from a trusted source and was so intrigued by the 'fact' that she told others about it. Her belief was easily started and then reinforced in her own mind each time she told someone else the same story. It is also possible that the belief was further reinforced by another belief – what if she didn't want to be caught spreading rumors or untruths after holding something out to be true? Her belief of not being someone who spreads rumors may have caused her to fully believe the story once she related it because if the story were false that would mean (according to her other belief) she was guilty of spreading rumors.

I would venture to say most if not all of us have fallen prey to believing bad information that is passed around guised as a fact, which just goes to show you how easy it is to form and reinforce a belief. Forming a belief only requires that you:

1. Choose the belief you want
2. Put that belief into your thought process as often as possible, and
3. Reinforce the belief with valuable examples.

Believing You Can Change

Here's a fact to consider: humans have the power to change any belief at any time. This fact is evidenced by how fast we change our beliefs when we go through a traumatic experience, when we are confronted with proof of the unreal, when we are reminded of something we once believed but lost touch with over time. The fact is that anyone can change. The problem is what we believe and how we think determines how we view our individual power to change our beliefs. Some don't believe they can change their belief. It's ironic because the single belief of **not believing** they can change forms their reality and they are stuck: they truly cannot change!

Do you believe you can change? If not, it's time for you to start the process over and find the motivational desire to believe you can change and then begin forming the belief that you can change. When it comes to changing something about yourself, if you don't believe you can make the change, you never will. It is imperative that you consciously believe you can make the change.

At this stage, we've discussed finding the desire to change and believing you can change. Please don't worry about 'how' you're going to make the change – all you need at this stage is to **believe**

you can change regardless of the 'how'. The methods for changing are what the rest of this book is about, but those steps are pointless until you believe you can change.

Depending on the change you want to make, this part can be difficult. Sometimes what you're trying to change will seem so impossible you just won't believe you can make the change. Other times, another one of your beliefs will stop you from thinking you can make the change (e.g. perhaps you can't change because you believe the change will go against your family traditions or culture). Whether you think making the change will be difficult or simple is only a measurement of the effort you think it will take to change. If you think the effort is difficult, then congratulations: you at least believe you can change given enough effort.

Probably everyone at some point in their life feels like a victim or powerless to change themselves to achieve what they want. I know I have. But that feeling is just a feeling and not a fact, which means we also have the power to start feeling we **can** change and that we **are** powerful, not powerless.

Say this phrase to yourself: "I believe I can change myself". When you say it, do you feel good or bad? If you felt positive feelings by saying that phrase, then you probably do believe you can change and should continue working on the behavior you're trying to change. If you felt silly, stupid, insecure, fake or as though you are lying to yourself, then that's an indication you don't believe you can change, and that's the first belief you should work on while you read this book. Your first task is to choose to believe you can change yourself.

Does this sound like the chicken before the egg problem? How can you change if you don't believe you can change? That's the real magic of this methodology: it works when you follow the steps. When you start by building the desire to change (i.e. when you at least want to believe you can change yourself) you are building up strength and finding reasons to create the belief. Then when you use the tools in this chapter, you will begin to feel empowered. The next steps will show you a straight-forward method to break down the walls that are holding you back. Before you know it, you will truly believe you can change and you'll be prepared to tackle any other changes you want to make.

Chapter 4

Strength is defined by the conversation you have with yourself during difficult situations

Step 3: Unlock Your Beliefs

To change yourself means to change your beliefs and emotions towards facts. This step shows you how to begin understanding what these beliefs and emotions are towards your current behavior and the underlying causes of that behavior (so you can choose to change them).

Start by asking yourself intelligent questions, the kind of questions that will allow you to probe your brain without anyone judging you or guiding your thoughts. The reason change typically doesn't last for most people is because they never go through this process, mostly because they didn't know such a process existed or was even necessary. So let me show you how to do it.

I'm assuming you have a specific behavior or facet about yourself you want to change. Perhaps someone told you you're always negative and you don't want to be 'that' person. Or maybe you find yourself constantly seeking approval from a parent. Maybe you want to learn a new brain power like waking up on time without an alarm clock. Whatever the behavior you want to adopt you need to understand why you're either doing the opposite behavior now or not performing the new behavior.

To begin to understand your beliefs you need to ask a question and consider the answers. I want to emphasize that this process is entirely up to you – you are the only one asking questions and you are the only one answering the question, nobody else. So don't be embarrassed to ask yourself a really intimate or otherwise unsettling question (e.g. "what is causing me to not be able to urinate in a public restroom"). For each question you ask, you will probably come up with lots of answers, so write them down. For each answer you come up with, you must ask one really important question: Is this answer the root cause of your current behavior?

What you're trying to do in this step is identify the root cause of your behavior. That cause may go all the way back to your childhood and may require you to ask more questions about ancillary behaviors or answers that result from your first question. Think of this like a tree where your current behavior is a single leaf on the end of a branch. Each time you ask a question and answer it, you have the ability to go up the branch and either connect with other branches and end up at other leaves, or continue down the branch to the trunk of the tree and roots where everything comes from.

I personally find this journey fascinating because when you're honest with yourself in how you answer your own questions and when you consider the possibilities, you start to realize how big your tree, your reality, really is and how it is constructed.

The Kinds Of Questions To Ask Yourself

Previously I mentioned that your brain will always answer a question it is asked. It's true - try it! Next time you lose your car keys ask your brain where you put them and your brain will start telling you. Now be careful, you may get more than one answer. Our thoughts can interrupt our brain's attempt to give us the straight answer by giving directives and judgments instead of constructive answers. For example, if you lose your car keys and ask your brain "where did I leave my car keys", a natural reaction is to come up with creative suggestions to look for the keys, like "go look by your wallet where you always keep them" or "check the car, Dummy, you always leave them in the ignition", etc.

When asking yourself a question, try to listen for just the answer. Listening to the directives will effectively short-circuit your brain and you will get more than the single answer you need. Try to quiet your thoughts, ask the question and wait for an answer. The answer will come to you like a memory, a memory of where you put the car keys, and that's how you'll know you're getting a real answer.

I suppose someone's going to stop me after trying this exercise and tell me, "I tried asking myself where I put the car keys but I kept getting wrong answers". It's true that not all the answers are the best ones for your question, but they are all real answers. Please notice that the question I suggested you ask, "where did I leave my car keys" isn't very specific. Your brain can remember lots of times and places where you left your keys, which may or may not be the last place you left them. This is why the kind of question you ask yourself, and how you ask it, is very important. If you want the right answer, you have to ask the right question. Try asking "when was the last time I had my car keys today" or "where was the last place I had my car keys today". The first answer may not be the correct one, but with practice listening to your answers, you will become very good at finding the correct answer faster…and your keys.

The kinds of questions you should be asking need to be very specific to what you are trying to change about yourself. Each question should be direct, as exact as possible, and open-ended. I suggest you start with the following questions by including a phrase about the actual behavior, and then expand on these questions as you become comfortable with this approach:

1. What causes me to behave/not behave the way I do?
2. How do I feel when I behave in that way?
3. Who does my behavior affect?
4. When do I behave in the way I do?
5. Where or in what circumstances do I behave in that way?

These are not the only questions to ask, but they are a great starting point. Let's put them in context with a real-world example. As an example, perhaps I'm afraid to give friends and even family members a hug when I greet them and want to change to be more friendly and affectionate. Here are the questions I would ask myself:

1. What causes me to feel afraid to give a hug?
2. How do I feel when I don't give a hug?
3. How do I feel when I do give a hug?
4. Who is affected when I don't give a hug?
5. When do I find myself afraid of greeting someone with a hug?

One question I haven't asked is "why am I afraid to give hugs?" Why questions are often easier to come up with than the other types but they have a potentially negative side effect: a natural tendency to answer these questions with judgments instead of real answers. Questions that start with "why" are valid questions and you can definitely ask them, but be careful not to accept answers that aren't constructive. For example, the answer to the above why question could be "because I'm afraid I smell bad" or "because I feel awkward". Why questions often cause our brains to answer with judgments based on how we feel about ourselves at the moment (e.g. "because nobody wants to give me a hug" or "because I don't deserve to be hugged").

When you ask a question that starts with how, what, when, where, who (instead of why), you're forced to think about the cause and effect, and not just provide yourself with reactive responses or self-judgments. The idea is to find constructive answers and to help yourself, not beat yourself up.

Exploring The Obvious Reasons For Your Actions

When you ask yourself a question about why you do the things you do, the right answer is probably your first answer. Seems easy, but our thoughts clutter our mind and stop us from believing our gut reaction. Part of this process, as you do it more often, will teach you to listen to your instincts and trust your initial reaction in all areas of your life. Having used this process now for over twenty years, I have become very adept and comfortable with changing my beliefs to affect the changes I want. In many cases I can re-program myself in a few minutes or a few hours (instead of weeks or months) by listening to my gut and tracing the paths of my questions and answers to the root cause. The key is to learn to listen to your instinct and most accurate answer to your question.

An Example Of Seeing Clarity Through Emotion

I mentioned earlier that my father was addicted to drugs when I was a kid. That was when I was four and also when my parents divorced. As a result of that divorce my mother went on welfare, we shared our house with another family to afford the rent, and we began to rebuild our lives. My childhood took on an adventurous turn every year as we moved nearly every year of my life to new schools, new homes in new cities/states and making new friends over and over again. At face-value, many people have viewed my childhood as challenging, chaotic, negative and wonder why I didn't end up in jail and/or on drugs. Fortunately, due to the strength and outlook of my mother and family, I have never viewed my past with any negativity or remorse. Sure, it was challenging at times, as all childhoods are for every child, but I never chose to focus on the negative.

The reason I bring this up is to highlight the one result that had become negative for me, which was my relationship with my father. At age 19, I decided to live with my father during my summer break from college because I hadn't done that since I was four and wanted to know who he was. I remember when I confronted him about our past and his lack of presence in my life. It was a tough conversation, one I did not look forward to and one that took many agonizing days to find the courage to bring up. Fortunately, my father, being a substance abuse counselor, was an excellent listener and was aware of who he was and who he had become at that moment. After I had my say and asked him the tough questions I needed clarity on, he gave me straight-forward and honest, not-proud, answers. I was then faced with a decision: do I forgive him or not? Frankly, the decision was truly whether or not I forgave myself for my feelings.

If you think about this situation the way I did at the time, you'll see that his actions/inactions in the past were the facts in my life. Therefore, to feel better, the only aspect I controlled and could change was my beliefs and my thoughts about those facts. Using this methodology took a few hours to internally work through my questions and answers, and I immediately began to undo the hurt I had felt to that point. Of course this event was a huge emotional release and a big break-through for me that to this day deeply strengthens the relationship I have with my father. To fully let go of the pain certainly took longer than a few hours, but making the change to allow the pain to release is what's important and that part didn't take long at all.

With this example of my relationship with my father, what was the crux of my pain? I actually used this process twice with my father: once to bring myself to the point where I could talk to him, and a second time to change how I felt about our relationship. To understand how to approach him I first had to understand what was bothering me. There were lots of ways I could look at what I felt:

- Was it that he hadn't been present in my life?
- Was it that I couldn't relate to him because we were so different?
- Was I afraid of growing up to become my father?
- Was I upset about what his drug abuse did to my life?
- Was I bothered that I didn't have a traditional father?
- Was I hurt that he hadn't acted like a traditional father-figure for me?
- Was I unsure about what role he wanted to play in my life going forward?

I asked these and many other questions. Then I looked for the most obvious one, which was that I felt he wasn't a traditional father-figure for me and that was how I confronted him. Certainly I asked him questions about the drugs, how he saw himself at that time in my life and what his reasons were for not being a larger part of my life as I grew up. All these questions contributed to the base problem that I didn't feel like he was my father; that he hadn't earned that role. By gaining clarity on what was truly bothering me I was allowed to have a more direct and honest conversation with him and to get the answers I needed most.

How To Identify The Obvious Answer

All of the questions I have listed here are valid and any one of them may seem like the 'obvious' answer to an outside observer. But for me, the one that was obvious was easy to spot because it conjured up the most emotion when I asked it and I could feel it had the deepest roots out of the other questions. As you look at this scenario with clarity of mind and when you're not struggling with the level of emotion I was struggling with at the time, you might also notice that not feeling like he had been a father to me is really the result of all the other questions I asked (e.g. not being present, taking drugs, not wanting to be like him, not being able to relate to him, etc). In this case, the obvious answer is also the most logical answer.

To speed up this process of exploring the root cause of your behaviors, focus your questions and pinpoint the most relevant answers. To spot the most obvious reason or cause out of all the questions and answers you list, listen to your gut and measure the weight of the pain or emotion you feel in relation to that question or answer. If you feel all of your questions and answers weigh the same for you then there may not be one distinct reason, but a combination of many. However, in many situations you will find one or two reasons that are much more powerful than others and those are the reasons you should start with as you go on to the next step.

As you assess the change you want to make, don't discount the most obvious reason for why you behave the way you do. The most obvious reason may not be the root cause of your behavior, but it is probably the fastest path to find the root cause, and finding the root cause is the point of this step. Once you find it you'll be able to move on to the last step in this process, which is to choose to change. But before you move on to the next step, let's further discuss how to get to the root cause.

Finding The Root Cause

The root cause is the earliest point in your life where you feel a decision, event or emotion has caused a belief and/or series of supporting beliefs and thoughts to form and result in your current behavior. You might think that you smoke because it's a habit and you're addicted. But if you think all the way back to the time when you started smoking, what was the reason then? If you look at that reason and go back to the point where that reason began, you'll eventually find the root cause of smoking.

I don't want to belabor this point, but why is finding the root cause so important in this process? Have you ever killed a weed in your garden? You can't just cut the top off because the roots are still there and will grow out again. The only way to completely get rid of a weed is to get the roots out. Your brain works the same way. Quitting smoking can be done physically and chemically, but the habit or desire to smoke won't go away without eliminating the belief and emotion driving it. The strength behind all of your actions resides with your core beliefs.

I have never been a smoker, so I don't want to trivialize a change that I can only imagine to be painfully difficult to make. But if you ask yourself questions and review your answers for why you smoke, and trace it back to before you started smoking, you can find the underlying event that started you on the path to smoking.

What if you found out that you associated the concept of smoking with being an adult? That reason, if true for you, doesn't mean you wanted to smoke or agreed with the principles behind it at the time, but it does show a motivation to start and continue smoking. In this example, your core belief for your current behavior is smoking will make you feel like an adult. Assuming you're an adult now, does smoking actually provide that feeling? If not, then you can choose to eliminate or change that original belief (which is the subject of the next chapter).

If you can identify the root cause then you have the choice to eliminate or change the belief that was formed at that point. Keeping with this example, if you suddenly believed that smoking did NOT make you feel more like an adult then you will be removing a key piece of the structure supporting your current behavior. Destroying that one component of your foundation may, by itself in some cases, be enough to have a domino-effect on the rest of your behavior immediately enabling you to change the current behavior. At a minimum, finding your core belief will allow you to start making changes.

Exercise: To Find The Root Cause

Finding a root cause of a behavior is an iterative process. Like peeling back the layers of an onion, this exercise will have you question your behavior and come up with an answer to your own question. As you do this, think of it like drilling down from the leaf on a tree to a branch to the tree trunk to the roots. For each answer you give to your question you will start again and question each of your answers. Since an answer to your probing question can provide detail about the behavior, questioning an answer can provide detail about what lead to that answer. Repeating this process will drive towards the root cause.

To find your root cause:

1. Ask probing questions about your current behavior
2. Answer each probing question and identify the primary reason(s) to your current behavior by reviewing each answer
3. Now ask more probing questions about the primary reason(s) you identified in the last step

4. Again, identify the most obvious or emotional reason(s) by reviewing each answer from step 3

5. Continue repeating steps 3 and 4 for your answers, digging deeper on each repetition until you discover the event or core belief that lead to your behavior

You'll know you found the root cause when you can no longer ask any questions or come up with any answers to questions. As you ask questions and focus on the answers that most likely lead to the root cause, you will eventually reach a point where there aren't any questions to ask. Or you may simply find a belief you're not willing to change.

For example, let's say you want to be more assertive and not let people walk all over you. As you trace through your beliefs for why you are not more assertive or why you let people take advantage of you, perhaps your questions and answers lead you back to a time when someone was kind to you and gave to you freely. If you viewed that person's giving as an attribute you wanted to aspire to would you want to change what you believe about that person's gesture, that they are kind? In other words, do you want to change your current behavior by changing how you feel about being kind in general? Probably not because being kind is a good, positive attribute that is central to who you are. But this point may be your root cause or core belief that lead to "being kind to a fault".

Up to this point, I have been showing you the process of asking questions and getting to the root cause. What I haven't said directly is that by asking a question and getting an answer, you're actually discovering each belief underlying your behavior. Each answer is a potential belief that you carry and use. As you move through each level of questioning, you uncover more levels to your belief system which help you see why you act a certain way. When you get to the root cause of your behavior, what you're really finding is your core belief that affects all the other beliefs in sequence. A leaf on a tree doesn't exist without roots sending water up through the trunk, out along its branches all the way out to the leaf. Nor does your reality exist without a core belief guiding a fact through your beliefs and related thought processes.

I know from experience that finding a single core belief isn't always possible, nor am I always ready and willing to look that deep. Even if you don't find your core belief, you can still change yourself. I highly recommend that you do everything you can to recognize the deepest part of your belief system affecting your life, but you don't have to. I have made many lasting changes by eliminating or modifying higher-level beliefs. But finding your core beliefs and making changes at that level will greatly increase your chances of creating a long-lasting result.

Think of making changes to yourself the same way you make changes to your house. Over time you can decorate your house differently, paint it different colors, upgrade fixtures, etc. All of these additions add to the overall appearance and quality of the house just like you take on new beliefs over time to hopefully become the person you want to become. But if you decide to change something serious, like the plumbing or electrical, you will need to strip back the surface of your house and get to the foundation to make those types of changes. When it comes to changing serious behaviors, you'll need to strip back the layers of beliefs to find your core beliefs if you want to make real, long-lasting changes.

Now… with your analysis done, your beliefs identified, your root cause out in the open and your motivational desire pushing you to become who you want to be, the time has come to change.

Changing means you get to pick and choose the beliefs you want. This last step is like a shopping spree for your brain and money is no object.

Chapter 5

Happiness is always worth the risk

Step 4: Design Your Reality

When I was a kid, everyone in my family liked olives except me. I could never understand how my brother could put black olives on his fingertips and then eat them like they were candy. They weren't candy! They were salty and gross. They smelled bad. Worst of all, their texture was weird. How could anyone like olives?

It wasn't until I was in my mid-20's that I decided that I wanted to see why people liked olives so much. This decision actually came about because my curiosity about mushrooms was piqued by a gentleman sitting next to me in first class on a business flight. He was in his mid-50's and was returning from a three-week vacation in France where he went truffle and mushroom hunting. I was stunned – people spend their vacations hunting for mushrooms? Are you kidding me?!? I asked him what was so compelling about mushrooms that he could spend his vacation looking for them. For the next hour he told me more than I ever thought I could know about fungi.

I was fascinated. Here was a world I didn't even know existed focused on one delicacy. I wondered how someone could create such a refined sense to appreciate all the different types of mushrooms. I thought appreciating mushrooms must be a lot like appreciating wine. As you get older and more experienced in tasting wine, even taking lessons on wine, you start to sense and enjoy the nuances and hidden flavors.

But how was I going to enjoy mushrooms? After 25 years of trying all types of food, I still had not learned to like mushrooms. I then turned my attention to olives because, like mushrooms, there are lots of varieties but perhaps less complexity (at least in my mind). For me olives were the lesser of the two evils and probably easier to come to terms with first. So I decided to start working on changing my beliefs about olives. Having already succeeded in liking fish, I felt I could use this method for reprogramming my mind to actually enjoy olives and perhaps later attempt mushrooms. My motivational desire was fairly simple and not highly emotional because I had nothing to lose by changing or staying the same. My motivational desire was two-fold: curiosity to see the world in a way that others do, and sheer interest in exploring how powerful the mind is to affect change.

With my desire in place, and the belief that I could pull this off, I started by asking questions and analyzing my reasons for not liking the olives. It didn't take me long to realize that most of what I didn't like about olives were trivial reasons that could be changed very easily. I had reasons like:

- I didn't like the smell
- I didn't like the saltiness
- I didn't like the texture
- I didn't like the taste

As I looked at each of these and other reasons for disliking olives, I then thought about how much I actually did like many of these factors. For example, I love olive oil in my salads and in cooking, so why didn't I like the taste of olives? When I traced the reasons further back to my childhood when my sense of taste was far simpler and far more susceptible to disliking strong tastes, I realized I formed a belief to **not** like the taste of olives. But as an adult, I actually did like the taste and the belief was no longer valid, but psychologically, that belief kept telling me I didn't like olives.

All I did, and what I'm showing you to do, is choose to feel and believe differently about each reason for my current behavior. If I didn't like olives because of a belief about taste that I formed a long time ago, especially a belief that was no longer valid, then I could change the belief. Changing the belief requires first, to recognize the belief exists, second, understand why the belief exists and third, choose a belief to replace the existing belief. In my case, I discovered the belief that I didn't like the taste of olives. I then understood that I formed that belief as a child with limited knowledge and understanding. Lastly, I chose the belief to "like olives" to replace the old belief.

The last step, replacing the old belief with a new one, can be as simple as seeing yourself swap out the belief in your head, like watching a plumber pull out a bad piece of pipe and insert a new one. Or it can be as complex as revisiting that core belief every time you are faced with the old behavior. For me that meant each time I saw an olive and felt the reaction of not liking olives I had to remind myself I had a new belief that I LIKED olives, and the old belief was no longer valid.

It did take a few weeks to really, truly like olives. The challenge I faced was that there were so many different kinds of olives to try and I had not formed opinions about every kind out there. However, by changing my belief to like olives, I had a new-found interest in trying them all. I started this change while on a trip to Spain and Portugal where I was served different olives with nearly every meal. I was able to try dozens of different types of olives in just a few weeks, some varieties I loved and some I didn't like at all.

Keep in mind that my goal wasn't to fall in love with olives and enjoy every kind out there. My goal was to like olives in general. The difference was that my new belief now allowed me to explore the world of olives and to achieve my goal of discovering what people see in them. I still don't like the big, green, salty olives, and prefer the smaller, sweeter varieties. But I will now try any olive and in most cases honestly enjoy it.

Choose How You Want To Feel About The Root Cause

The final step in this process of changing yourself is to choose what you want to believe. It starts with your root cause and core belief. Assuming you used the prior step to identify the lowest-level belief, now you can choose to change or not change. You won't always want to change a core belief, and nor should you. To figure out if you should change a belief there are three questions to ask yourself, in this order:

1. What is the most effective belief for you?
2. How will changing the belief affect your other behaviors?
3. Do you want to change the belief?

The first step is to look at your belief and ask yourself what is the most effective belief for you. Since a core belief of mine was "I did not like the taste of olives", my first task was to ask myself if the current belief was the most effective belief in order to reach my goal of enjoying olives. This is an easy example because the core belief (not liking olives) directly contradicted the result I wanted (to like olives). I DID want to like olives, so a more effective belief would be to change the core belief from "dislike" to "like" in regards to olives. From a more complicated example, when I wanted to eliminate jealousy I asked myself which belief would be the most effective one: to remain jealous or to eliminate jealousy.

Before I made that decision, I went through the second step by asking myself this question: **how will changing this belief affect other behaviors?**

If I chose to like olives, would I change another behavior in the wrong way? Not really... I surmised that the worst thing that would result from this change could be a cupboard full of olives.

Now I had found a more effective belief to adopt and I had asked whether or not the new belief would help or hurt me. The third question of whether I want to change was easy to conclude: this was a change I was willing to embrace and adopt.

I like this example of changing my behavior about olives because learning to like a food seems really hard on the surface, but then becomes a lot simpler when you see that you only have to change one belief at a time. Anyone in my situation could replace the core belief of disliking olives with liking olives (keep in mind, this is a change I wanted to make and I had a motivational desire to change this belief).

What's even better is that when you apply these concepts towards changing even more complex behaviors, you'll find that each change is just as straight-forward. The only difference between types of changes is the amount of time it takes to determine what the root causes are and to assess each one.

This method of change works for two very big reasons: 1) you have a method for discovering your core beliefs, and 2) you only have to make one change to one belief at a time, not all of them at once. It's like eating an elephant… how do you eat an elephant? One bite at a time. How do you change yourself? One belief at a time.

If you take a difficult, emotion-driven behavior you want to change and find the core belief that the behavior stems from, you only have to choose to replace that one belief with the most effective belief you can come up with – the belief you want. When I think back to my childhood and realize my extreme focus on money came from a time when I was really poor and wanted to afford a soda, my outlook towards money became a trivial issue. As an adult, I can easily afford that soda so why do I have to continue holding onto a belief that I can't afford the soda? I'm an adult, so why hold onto a belief that was formed when I was only a child? That old belief no longer serves me so I changed it.

In some cases, changing the core belief will take a little more time to assess because of how much of an impact a new core belief can have on other behaviors. When I changed my belief about money, I chose a belief that maintains the positive qualities I have (ambition, generosity, respect for the value of money, etc.) and eliminated the negative qualities (seeking money at the cost of happiness, using money as power, etc). I could have easily chosen a belief that was so extreme that I would lose my ambition, generosity or even create new negative traits like a total disregard for the value of money. As you review your core beliefs and choose to change them or not, choose a new belief that will complement your strengths and eliminate your weaknesses.

Changing your core belief is not the last step in this process, nor will it be the only belief you challenge and choose to keep or change. The core belief is the first to consider changing and you do not always have to replace it in order to achieve the change you want. You may decide that the core belief is a good, solid foundation that you rely upon and do not want to modify. That is perfectly fine and I have done that many times myself. But now you can start changing the rest of your beliefs to fully affect your behavior.

Change The Beliefs Leading From The Core

In step 3 you spent your time asking questions about your behavior and finding potential reasons to explain it. As you assessed each reason by asking additional questions, you discovered reasons behind those reasons. Continuing along, you should have built a whole series of branches from your behavior back to your core belief. In fact, if you put your current behavior on paper and drew a line from the behavior through each reason and sub-reason and it's sub-reasons, your drawing would start to resemble a tree branch or several branches.

Each one of those branches or reasons actually represents a belief that contributes to your current behavior ultimately forming your reality. To change your reality, you must change your beliefs – perhaps all of them along the way. You already started with the core beliefs. The next step is to move up to the next branch or reason and choose to change that belief or keep it. Once you assess that belief, you'll move up the branch to the next one until you reach your behavior. Then, if you have other branches and core beliefs to resolve, you work on those until you have worked on them all.

Affecting change in this manner does require you to look at and possibly change all of the beliefs that impact your behavior. The more beliefs you have, the longer this process can take. But don't be discouraged. This process doesn't have to be done all at once – you can work on one belief today and then move up the branch to the next belief in a few days or weeks when you feel you've established the new belief.

One of the benefits of working on your core belief first is that if you change it, you should find it progressively easier to change your related beliefs too. The new core belief may already invalidate the next belief up the branch, making the entire set of beliefs that resulted from the core belief obsolete, like sawing off a branch at the trunk instead of trimming each twig and little branch first.

At the end of this book, is an example to show you how the process works from end-to-end. If these steps for changing beliefs aren't completely clear yet, the fully-explained example should help. But before we get there, it's worthwhile to discuss how to ensure the new belief becomes permanent.

Making The New Belief Stick

When my father recovered from his drug and alcohol abuse he became a substance abuse counselor. His unique background of having been a minister of a church and doing marriage counseling, combined with his experience of getting himself off drugs, enables him to help others with their addictions. I have sat in on his counseling classes and discovered that he is amazing at what he does. I have also seen him take his own advice, which taught me some things about addiction and recovering from addiction.

This book is not intended to treat serious addictions, though I imagine this process could be effective for some people in addition to other treatments. There is one aspect of recovering from addiction, however, that is very relevant to this process, which is how to make the change stick. When my father decided to quit smoking after 20 years, he shared with me the process of how to stop while he was doing it. I got to watch and see him do it over time and measure the results for myself. He was successful and did stop smoking.

My father's choice to stop smoking was related to his health. He went into the hospital for nine days due to heart problems. That was nine days of absolutely no smoking. By the time he walked out of the hospital his mind was made up to quit. While his cravings were already subsiding to some degree and he had a method for handling the cravings, he now faced a very tough problem: changing the habits associated with smoking.

On the first day back from the hospital, he sat down in his reclining chair to watch TV and instinctively reached for a cigarette. While there was still a part of him that was addicted to the cigarette, the real driving force to get one was the sheer habit of smoking in that chair while watching TV. If he was going to beat smoking, he had to beat the habit of smoking, not just the chemical addiction.

Habits Are The Longest Lasting Changes

The lesson my father taught me from that experience was how he dealt with the habit. He didn't deny himself the cigarette – in fact he kept a pack and a lighter by his side at all times! Instead of trying to deny the habit he recognized the exact point in time where his habitual behavior exhibited itself: watching TV, waking up, going for a walk, driving his car, etc. Each time the event occurred he made a choice to smoke or not to smoke.

Making any change last comes down to making a single choice to not use the old behavior when it naturally begins to occur. Each time you make that choice you are choosing if you want to change or not. If your motivational desire is strong enough, if you understand your beliefs and chose to change them, and if you recognize that the behavior is now relegated to a habit you want to break, then your permanent change will be the result of you choosing the new behavior each time you recognize the habit.

Recall from step two that your reality is the result of how your thoughts use your beliefs to interpret facts. Your goal is to create your new reality with new behavior. Since you have already identified the beliefs that caused the old belief and changed them to support the new belief, the only piece left is new thought processes. These thought processes are best defined by your habits.

There are several types of thought processes we rely on in our daily lives:

- Conscious thoughts
- Subconscious thoughts
- Habits or automatic thoughts

Conscious thoughts are the conversations you have in your head, your inner dialogue as you assess situations and think about things. Certainly if you are to create a lasting change your conscious thoughts need to reflect your new behavior, but this has already been handled! Changing your core and related beliefs has laid the foundation for your conscious thoughts to change systematically and automatically without much conscious effort.

Remember, beliefs are the rules your brain uses to interpret facts. That means your mind will now use your new chosen belief as a rule to create your thoughts, resulting in conscious thoughts that support your belief. As an example, if you chose to believe that money does not equal happiness, then your inner conversations about money will now create a stream of conscious thoughts that follow rules around money not equating to happiness.

Another form of thought is the subconscious ones that happen without our awareness and knowledge. Those thoughts are a book unto itself, and are best tapped into through the other two types of thoughts. We'll leave that topic alone for now. The remaining type of thought is your habits or automated thoughts.

Habits are a combination of your conscious and subconscious thoughts working together to form your actions in a rhythmic, automated manner. Since I'm not going to delve into the world of subconscious thoughts, we're left with the portion of habits that are conscious. The conscious thoughts that accompany the habit are all the thoughts and conversations you have to reinforce why you're doing the habit. As you form a habit, these conversations are usually in the form of a justification ("I'm just watching TV to wind down", "watching TV is a nice way to relax after a hard day of work", "I can't fall asleep at night unless I watch a little TV", etc.). When the habit is well-formed, the conscious thoughts are usually pretty quiet because it doesn't take much, if any, conversation in your head to perform the habit. You probably don't say to yourself, "oops, I didn't watch TV yet, so I better go do that so I can go to bed", you just do it as a matter of routine.

To break a habit, you have to deal with the thoughts that relate to it. This is easy now because your conscious thoughts have already begun to rework themselves by virtue of your new belief. The result is when you go to perform the habit your thoughts will no longer be aligned with the habit and your new conscious thoughts will start making themselves heard. It is these new, louder, inner dialogues that are going to help you deal with the other part of your habit, the subconscious part.

It's not important how or why our subconscious works, it is only important that these thoughts drive our habitual nature. To change them we need to realign those thoughts to follow our beliefs. In a way, our habits are like little programs that are running in our brain and they need to be re-written and re-programmed. This is best done by first changing your beliefs that support the original habit (which you've done) and, second, by using your conscious thoughts to eliminate or realign the habit altogether.

Have you ever made a magnet from a needle or paperclip? Changing a habit is very much the same thing. To make a simple magnet, take out a needle and a small magnet (like a refrigerator magnet). Take the magnet and stroke the needle in one direction over and over again 30 to 50 times. It's like petting a cat – repeatedly in only one direction. Over time, the magnet will cause the atoms in the needle to all align in the same direction, which then turns the needle into a small magnet.

Your habits are like the atoms of a needle: a set of subconscious thoughts arranged in an unknown order that result in a habit. To change the habit, use your conscious thoughts to continually stroke the habit in a different direction until it changes and aligns with your beliefs. Each time your habit appears your conscious thoughts that don't align with the habit will also appear, becoming louder and asking you what you're doing (e.g. "why am I reaching for a cigarette when I don't believe in smoking?" or "why did I turn on the TV if I don't need it in order to fall asleep?" or "why do I keep eating when I'm already full?"). That is your opportunity to choose to support the new belief with a new thought process and a new habit. Each time you choose the new thoughts over the habit, you'll be using your conscious thoughts like a magnet to stroke the habit into a new alignment.

Keeping Your New Belief

Everything we've discussed is related to one single notion: how to change. While the process started with helping you find the desire and belief to change, the actual process of changing is a matter of identifying what to change and what to change it to. We used your desire and belief as the fuel to drive the engine of change. We have also reviewed the different kinds of thought processes that drive your behavior, including how to change your habits. The only thing left is to make sure that the change lasts for as long as you want it to last. Now it's time to use the fuel of your desire and belief to continue driving your change and holding it in place.

In my experience, if I have fully adopted the beliefs I want and have the desire to challenge my habits and change them, making the new change last is fairly easy. This process of change has the wonderful side-effect of creating self-awareness. Becoming aware of your beliefs, thoughts and habits opens you up to a whole new way to view the world. Each time you are faced with your old behavior, whether it is exhibited by you or someone else, you will be acutely aware of the behavior, the reasons why you changed it and your new belief. As long as you choose to reinforce your new belief by acknowledging the new vs. the old, you will naturally keep the changes you make.

Keeping a change in place is like driving down the freeway. Every now and then you check to see if you're heading in the right direction and reaffirm to yourself that you are. At any time, you have the power to change directions, even returning to the old behavior if you want to (and sometimes that is necessary and warranted). Unlike most recipes for change, this one does not require you to penalize yourself for failure or set up failure points in the first place. This isn't like a diet where you feel like you're cheating if you eat a cookie. This is more of a lifestyle where if you eat that cookie it's because you chose to do so in full awareness of the consequences, if any.

Dieting is another extremely interesting topic that I don't want to go too far into because I don't have a lot of experience with it. However, I recently spent four months monitoring my body fat changes to see how my diet and exercise affected things. I found that the more strict I became with my diet and the more rigorous my workouts became, the less results I achieved – the more balanced my diet and workouts became, the more success I had achieving my goals. It seemed contradictory! If I skipped the fast food and worked out twice a day, I was worse off than working out once a day and occasionally having my favorite burrito.

Your behaviors react in very much the same manner as your body does to your daily regimen. The more strict you become and the more you punish yourself for failing to change, the less likely your change will last vs. the more balanced you become and the more you reward yourself for the right behavior, the more successful your change will be. For example, (assuming you are not dealing with an eating disorder and need professional help) if you want to change your eating habits you don't have to cut out every cookie in order to change. By changing your beliefs, thoughts and habits related to the way you eat, you can still choose to eat your favorite cookie, perhaps in less quantity than before but you can still enjoy them in the context of your new lifestyle.

The simple answer to making your change last is to choose to believe in your new belief every chance you get.

Chapter 6

If you have to rationalize what you're doing, you're probably doing the wrong thing

The Victim's Roadblock To Change

It seems logical to me that every emotion has a specific purpose and the states of mind we find ourselves in as a result of one or more emotions is the natural progression of how we feel in general. It's when we become stuck or even dependent upon a certain emotional state that real problems arise. While we're given the tools to feel an emotion we sometimes lack the tools to stop feeling the emotion.

When I decided to stop feeling jealous I wanted to eliminate the emotion because I didn't feel I had the ability to control my actions and reactions once that emotion started. I became a victim of my own state of mind (a supposedly natural emotion). The challenge I unknowingly faced, before I even chose to change, was to determine whether the emotion of jealousy was occurring naturally or was perhaps fueled by other behaviors and ways of thinking. Fear, insecurity and perhaps a wild imagination was helping me feel jealous beyond any justifiable jealous reaction. I could understand feeling jealous if I watched my girlfriend kiss another guy or even flirt with another guy, but she never did that. Thus a twinge of jealousy sparked by an innocent gesture was blown out of proportion by my fear and insecurity, instead of kept in check by healthier reactions. Of course this is hindsight talking – I was not this aware at that time. All I knew is that I didn't like how I felt and I wanted a way to change it.

Why can't we change? Is it because we don't feel like we can? Are there too many reasons why we can't change? Is there someone who we think would be hurt if we did? How you answer these questions is an indication of whether you feel you're a victim to your current behavior or whether you know without a doubt that you can change. Then again, if you already know you can change, why haven't you? Even if you don't feel like a victim you are probably holding yourself hostage, holding yourself back from changing because of reasons, justifications or priorities you set ahead of making the change.

Three Types of Victims

When it comes to how we become victims there are really three main types of victims we become.

1. Victims Of Uncontrollable Circumstances
2. Victims Of Limiting Beliefs
3. Victims Of Procrastination

The first type, being subjected to uncontrollable circumstances, is truly outside ourselves and the circumstances affect us in ways that are debilitating. The other two are completely within our own minds and still keep us from reaching our goals. The challenge with being a victim, regardless of the type, is that victims believe they can't help themselves because they are literally a victim to circumstances beyond their control. All three types are within our power to overcome and change entirely, if we choose to and know how to.

Uncontrollable Circumstances

I've always believed that if you stuck me in a jail cell I would find a way to be happy. Perhaps that is simply an empowering belief that happiness can exist no matter what, but I tell you that belief to point out the idea of boundaries. Being in a jail cell, while certainly dire and undesirable at best, does offer a known set of boundaries. If you know the boundaries, what can and cannot happen, all you're left with is what's inside those borders to control for yourself (in this example, finding happiness). Uncontrollable circumstances are exactly this – a known set of boundaries beyond which you cannot control or change anything.

In dealing with a set of uncontrollable circumstances it is very easy for us to believe that because those circumstances are outside our ability to affect that nothing else can be changed. You can't change the fact that you're in prison or the fact that you're surrounded by metal and concrete, so what's left? Your reality is what's left. For some, being subjected to harsh circumstances means succumbing to the rules and facts instead of defining the reality they want. Fortunately, most of the situations we perceive to be uncontrollable can be highly affected by our actions, attitudes and efforts.

One of my favorite topics is career development, including how to ask for a raise and how to get the job you want. When I talk to most people about getting a raise or finding a new job, the first thing they do is tell me all the reasons why they cannot get the job or raise they want. Most people seem to look at their job as under the control of someone else. While I certainly respect that feeling, having been an employee who has had to look for a new job (I have been fired, laid off, merged, acquired and every other corporate method of losing a job) and who has asked for a raise many times, I have discovered that there are lots of ways in which to control these seemingly uncontrollable circumstances.

Getting past the feeling of being stuck in a situation beyond your control, getting past being a victim, starts with looking past the negative and limiting reasons inherent to the situation. It is true you might not get the job you want or the raise you ask for – that is a fact and facts are beyond your control. But what is within your control is how you ask for the raise, when you ask for the raise, why you ask for a raise, how often you ask for a raise, etc.

In college, when I was going in credit card debt each month just to buy groceries and gas, I felt I couldn't win. I worked 25 hours per week for a very successful stock broker. I studied long hours and received good grades, but not the best grades I was capable of. I always looked for ways to make more money, but no matter what, I kept going further in debt and struggled to survive. I was in serious need of finding a way to make more money.

After a few months of working at the stock brokerage, I decided to ask for a raise because that was one way to get more money to pay my bills. After I gathered the courage to sit down with my boss and ask for a raise, the answer was almost immediately no. My boss wasn't a jerk, rather he was a great guy who was running a business and he already paid me the top of the hourly wage range he had budgeted. Instead of rejecting my request out of hand he suggested I bring my homework to the office to work on during down times. That was more than fair of him, but it didn't help me pay my bills because I couldn't take on another job.

At that point in time, it would have been easy to simply accept these circumstances and assume there was nothing more I could do. Giving in to the circumstances is an honest answer and I wouldn't fault myself or anyone else for giving in. But when I find myself in difficult situations something inside of me causes me to work smarter (and harder) instead. As I walked out of the office that day, feeling dejected but not wanting to give up, I was struck by a thought: *a goal without action is merely a dream.*

That 'something' within me is the knowledge that uncontrollable circumstances are never beyond my influence if I can come up with a new approach and take action. Then I came up with a great idea: I could ask for a raise again. Why not? I already knew his answer was no so the worst that could happen is that he would say no again.

Except, next time I would do it differently and make it harder for him to say no.

On my second attempt to ask for a raise I came to my boss fully armed. Since the last time I asked for the raise I had worked harder and showed him my dedication, loyalty and effectiveness. I also showed up on time or early and left the office last. I proved that I was a valuable team member. I looked at my job through the perspective of being happy to have a job at all and being able to do homework there.

When I finally approached him again I referred to my work ethic, my proof, of why I deserved the raise. I even went so far as to tell him why I needed the raise (to pay for food, gas, and parking etc). My second attempt didn't go anywhere as he told me he'd think about it. A month later, my third attempt was a little better because when I told him I couldn't afford my expenses and might have to look for another job to make ends meet he gave me free parking at the office. It wasn't a cash raise but it did lower my expenses!

The fourth time I asked for a raise I finally got what I wanted. I approached him with the idea that I wanted to 'earn' the raise: the raise didn't have to simply be on my past merit or just a dollar-per-hour raise. How about a bonus structure based on my performance? He liked the idea a lot. A week later he came back with a counter-proposal that not only gave me a cash raise, but an incentive to do an even higher-quality job, a performance bonus for other tasks, and a small share in how well his business performed for the month. In total, the potential compensation was more than I had asked for. Even better, the assistant I worked directly under also received this bonus structure which improved her income.

Imagine what would have happened if I had just let my circumstances remain uncontrollable from my perspective.

Obviously I probably would not have received any increased compensation. Most likely I would have also had a poor attitude due to a victim mentality. Giving in to my circumstances would have definitely resulted in a bad work experience for me and my co-workers and may have even resulted in getting fired altogether.

It wasn't easy to look defeat in the eyes and decide to do the opposite of what I felt like doing – to work harder and ask for a raise until I got it. Believe me I felt defeated the first time I asked for a raise. I didn't want to go back to the office and pretend everything was ok. But I decided to not give up. I looked past the pain and found a direction that I felt could influence uncontrollable circumstances. Thankfully it worked.

I know from experience that there are far worse situations that fall into this category of uncontrollable circumstances and it is always easy to just continue being a victim and not changing. The challenge I offer to you when you find yourself in this situation is to stop looking at the negative reasons for why you won't succeed. Stop being a victim long enough to look for the possible reasons or ways in which you can succeed. You don't have to even know how you'll succeed because if you tell yourself that you're going to find a way, you will. Your brain will answer the question of "how can I get out of this situation" and show you how. Ask the question "how" and you'll stop being the victim of uncontrollable circumstances.

Limiting Beliefs

A limiting belief is any belief that limits your ability to grow, evolve or change. Believing you can't change is a limiting belief. Or perhaps you can't meet your dream guy until you lose weight. Or you can't get your dream job without a college degree. There are an infinite number of limiting beliefs out there and they all keep you as their victim. Like all smart captors they do their best to not let you see them until it's too late.

When I was 26 I started a software company. Within a few years the company started growing and we hired employees and opened up office space. I had done it... I had become the president of my own company. The only problem was that I was still under 30 years old. Why is that a problem? I had no idea, but it was a serious problem.

It wasn't until the day of my 30th birthday that it hit me. On that day I woke up and said, "Wow, I did it - I'm the CEO of a software company". Then this shallow sickness came over me, the painful awareness of a belief that I had held for the past four years for no good reason. For some reason, which I'll come back to, I had formed a simple belief that made me feel as though I was just some 'kid' who started a company and not the CEO, not a "President" that people would take seriously because I was so young.

I sat there in a stupor thinking about the countless conversations where I had discounted my own perspectives and the worth of my role in those conversations. How many people had I let myself feel inferior to? How many times did I undervalue myself? I'll never know how that belief truly held me back from success.

I was stunned that a limiting belief had been hiding for so long and then suddenly appeared. Thinking about it I realized that the limiting belief was "until I turned age 30, I would always be looked down upon by others as just some kid who started a software company". But that belief simply isn't true. There are countless CEOs who are under 30 and worth their weight in gold. Why wasn't I one of them? Because I didn't believe I could be, pure and simple.

I know why the belief formed and the reason was rather innocent. The belief formed as the result of a conversation I had with my mentor when I was 22 years old talking to him about a girl I was attracted to. I told him that she talked very highly of her ex boyfriend who owned his own software company and I didn't feel I could compete with that. In my defense, my mentor replied that "kids" under 30 who own a software business are a dime-a-dozen, there was nothing special about them and more likely, he was secretly a failure. That explanation made me feel better so I used it and ended up dating the girl. At the time I never imagined I would become the owner of a software company. Nor did I fathom that I would hold onto such a belief only to use it against myself later!

Lucky for me this particular belief had a built-in expiration date on my 30th birthday. But oh how I wish I could have seen it earlier. Which brings up the question, how to identify a limiting belief?

In my case I had never realized I was victim of a situation. Nor had I realized there was a change I should make. Running a company was my dream and I was doing it. I didn't believe I was a victim of anything, especially a belief. In other words, I wasn't looking to change and therefore wasn't looking at my beliefs.

To recognize a limiting belief you have to constantly assess what you believe and why. The process of change is what opens you up to seeing your beliefs. When you choose to change, regardless of what or how, you open yourself up to discovering all of your beliefs, including the limiting ones. The challenge you face in order to change is to overcome the feeling of NOT being able to change, feeling like a victim to your current circumstances. By acknowledging the feeling of being a victim could be one of three types, including a limiting belief, you are giving yourself the opportunity to recognize what is holding you back and make changes to that limiting belief.

Procrastination

This third type of being a victim is probably the one we're most familiar with and most despise. At least with the uncontrollable circumstances it's obvious the problem is outside our control. With procrastination it's totally our own fault and we know it. We beat ourselves up for it and use it as our crutch to explain away our failures. The truth is procrastination is just another belief, a belief that we can't do something now for any number of reasons. The best cure for procrastination is to change the belief to something empowering like "whenever I start a task I don't stop until it's done" or "when I say I'm going to do something, I always do it" or "I don't believe in procrastinating".

I have wanted to change my behavior towards receiving gifts for many years. It took several events during the past few months before writing this book, plus the justification that writing this book required me to show an in-depth look at this process, before I actually sat down to work on the change. When all is said and done, it only took a few hours to work out the beliefs behind my behavior and to make changes. If I can fix something in three hours that has caused countless hours of discomfort and grief throughout my life, why did I wait so long to do it? I'm human, just like you. I fell victim to my own mentality of "oh, it will work itself out" and "I don't have a good enough reason to make the change".

Whether we're looking at changing an emotional reaction, a habit or even trying to create a new behavior, we're always sitting on the edge of being empowered to change or becoming a victim trapped within our own mind. It is our very beliefs, thoughts and reality that keep us from making the change we want. In my career there have been times I put off doing a task because I believed the task would take me eight hours to complete. Then, when I had put it off for as long as possible and had to finally focus and get it done, it ended up taking only 30 minutes. Why did I wait so long to get it done? Because I <u>believed</u> it would take eight hours!

What beliefs are driving your procrastination to change? Try using this process to change your beliefs about procrastination. That one change alone can increase your effectiveness and happiness when doing things you currently dread.

What Victim Mentality Does To Those Around Us

There is no such thing as a beautiful victim. Nobody, other than victims, likes to side with the person who looks at the world as though the world owes them something. Nobody likes to be around victims because they choose to complain instead of change. Being a self-proclaimed victim is simply not pleasant for those who are not victims. We all work for our money. We all get hungry. We all sweat when it's hot. Or, as I like to say, even the wealthy sweat when it's hot outside.

The act of being a victim is completely self-centered. As a victim we are the center of the world and can see only the negative reasons for why we're stuck in our position. It's like standing in the middle of quicksand and every time we complain about sinking, we sink further. If you want out of quicksand, you lift yourself out by laying flat and swimming out. But like most who fall into quicksand our first instinct is to look for someone on the outside to save us.

What if the quicksand you're sinking in is your beliefs? Who can possibly save you from what you believe? Nobody can. Each of your beliefs either pulls you further, deeper into your reality of sinking and failing or helps prop you up to get out of the quicksand. What's worse is everyone around either gets sucked in too or they move away. Being a victim is nothing short of a downward spiral.

Victims are surrounded by three types of people:

1. Victims
2. Sympathizers
3. Empathizers

Victims always draw a crowd and all three types will come to see what's happening. As a victim, your worst enemy is the other victims that see a perfectly good hole to jump into so they can be a victim with you. Victims are so caught up in being a victim it often doesn't matter what they're a victim of. When you're a victim you spend your time telling everyone who will listen WHY you're a victim (when you should be figuring out how to change it). Victims dispense rationalizations and justifications for their situation as though their lives depend on it (well, at least their perception of reality depends on it). Other victims, who completely understand what it means to be a victim, love to jump in with you to commiserate, further weighing you down and dragging you under.

Sympathizers are those seemingly neutral parties who let you be a victim for as long as they can handle it. Either the Sympathizer doesn't know what to do, can't figure out how to help you or has been in your position and knows you need to release your pain somehow. It's always nice to have someone who will listen and coddle us when we're in pain. When you first display that pain to a Sympathizer, they'll be by your side for some time, but not forever. Eventually a Sympathizer will become aware of your negative outlook and either move away entirely, or turn into an Empathizer.

The Empathizer is your only potential savior when you're a victim. Empathizers are honest people you can trust to tell you what's actually happening. They're the ones on the side of the crowd yelling "Hey Dummy! Did you know you're sinking in quicksand?!?

Get out of there!!" Unfortunately, these are the people you ignore first and hear last.

When you first fall into your victim posture your first instinct is to look around and see who else is a victim. Like going back to see how big the crack in the side walk was that caused you to stumble, you're looking for another victim who will agree you were a victim of a poorly built sidewalk (instead of wondering if your shoes are too big or maybe you need to pick up your feet more when you walk). You rally support for why you are a victim so you don't have to admit you stumbled.

The next thing you do when becoming a victim is find more willing participants who will sympathize with you and hopefully become a victim too. It's not until you start to realize you're stuck and NEED to change that you look up and see the Empathizer.

Most of the time, I'm an Empathizer because I have a simple rule for dealing with victims: you, the victim, can complain to me about the same problem three times, after which if you're not making an effort to change the situation, I don't want to hear about it. I will only be your sympathizer for three complaints about the same problem, and then I'm going to be brutally honest with you. If you continue to complain without making attempts to change, be prepared for me to turn my back on you.

Victims hate this rule because I immediately show them that I will not commiserate with their plight and will not let them wallow in it in my presence. Victims beget victims. If I sympathize with a victim's position and encourage their complaining, instead of changing, they'll be forever stuck in the quicksand holding onto me like a lifeline. Personally, I refuse to leave my lifeline tied to a downward spiral. On the other hand, if you show me that you're fighting to change, looking for alternative ways out of your ordeal,

I'll let you complain as much as you want while you change because I know you're choosing to not be a victim any more.

Nobody is immune to becoming a victim – it happens to all of us. When it inevitably happens again the best thing to do is recognize it for what it is. Recognize who has joined you as a victim, who is merely placating you by listening to your condition and who is trying to help you by being honest and direct. It's the people who are being honest with you who are trying to help you get out of your victim mentality.

How To Not Be A Victim

The best course of action is to never be a victim. Obviously that requires you to believe that you'll never allow yourself to be a victim again. Until you form that belief, what you can start doing now is to immediately stop being a victim as soon as you're aware you've become one. If being a victim means to look only at the negative, to only speak in terms of your self-centered situation with justifications, and to want others to save you, then not being a victim is the opposite.

To not be a victim you need to look for the positive, to stop speaking in terms of why you are a victim and start speaking in terms of why you are NOT a victim. Not being a victim also means you stop waiting to be saved or looking for someone to save you. In other words, you take responsibility for yourself and seek to change yourself and your circumstances.

When I didn't get the raise the first time I asked for it my immediate reaction was to pity myself. I started looking at all the negatives… how difficult life was, how hard it was to be a student and work 20+ hours per week, how my grades could be better if I didn't have to work, how poor I was, etc., etc. The more negative thoughts I allowed, the more difficult it became to feel good and to see a way out of my predicament. Luckily for me I have an innate need to be happy (wait a minute, don't we all have this need?) and I stopped being a victim by looking at what I still had in my favor. I still had a job, which was a triumph to get in the first place! I did have a way to pay my bills (using credit cards) and I wasn't going to get kicked out of my apartment. I also had a car which allowed me to work off campus while many of my peers did not and could not work off campus where the higher paying jobs were.

A funny thing happens when you start to think about the positive: you stop feeling like a victim! Instead of being a victim with no hope for getting a raise, I started thinking about how I could still get a raise. That's when I came up with the idea to just ask for a raise once a month until I got it. It was such a simple solution I could only see once I began to look at things from a positive perspective.

The only person causing you to be a victim is you. It's your continuing rationalizations and justifications that keep you in your position. A rationalization may be as simple as thinking the person who got the job was 'luckier' than you.

I had a roommate who was continuously angry that he never sold one of his movie scripts, yet some 'no-talent' guy he knew from college was able to sell his scripts. Victims are always smarter than the non-victims and the supposedly stupid non-victims are just lucky. When you ask the victim what they've done to get the job, to sell the movie script, you'll find out they haven't done a thing since becoming a victim. They're waiting to be saved.

If you want to stop being a victim, stop waiting to be saved. Do the things successful people do. Lie on top of the quicksand and swim to the side. Write another script and try to sell it. Start dating again. Learn a new sport. Decide to change yourself. Decide to stop being a victim and move on.

Your victim mentality is controlled by you. You can choose to be a victim, attracting other victims, and sink to the bottom. Or, you can choose to be positive, choose to take action and choose to not be a victim. It starts with seeing the positive and, like the first raindrop to break a drought, you'll start to see your life come back to you. You'll send away the victims and realize the Empathizers in the crowd were your best friends all along.

Conclusion

Live up to your own standards:
no one else will do it for you

Become Your Best Self

If I can offer one belief to consider adopting, choose to believe in your best self. One thing I learned by moving to new schools every year as a kid is that nobody knows my potential better than I do. Deep down you know who you are capable of being too. Choose to believe in who you know you are and can become.

When you start to assess what you believe and choose the most empowering beliefs for you, your best self will naturally emerge. There is a fundamental truth that will safeguard you through this process: nobody will consciously choose a belief that harms them. Yes, we all unconsciously form limiting and debilitating beliefs. But when you see your beliefs clearly and have the choice, can you see yourself choosing a harmful one?

Certainly some beliefs are more empowering than others, but ultimately your goal, and the result of using my method for change, is to become your best self. Start now. Take the time to begin re-designing your reality through new beliefs and healthier thought processes and I know you will recognize your best self and become that person you've always wanted to be.

Make One Change At A Time

How does a six-year-old decide which toy to take out of the package and play with first at Christmas? They don't – they unpack ALL of their toys and leave them strewn across the floor to try and play with all of them at once. It's overwhelming!

Now that you have a new way to explore your beliefs and make changes, avoid being a six-year-old and toying with all your beliefs at once. Choose one and only one. Then work on that one change until you master it before moving on to the next. Invariably, as you go through this process, you're going to see lots of tangent beliefs you want to change. You'll be tempted to change them all at once, but don't. This process is intended to make one change at a time and if you make changes to tangent beliefs and behaviors before finishing the current one, you won't have an accurate way to know what changes are being made and what the results are. Plus, there is no need to overwhelm yourself with too many changes.

How do you eat an elephant? One bite at a time.

How do you change your reality? One belief at a time.

I wish you luck and success in making the changes you want. I'm confident you can make any change you want with this method. I look forward to hearing from you.

For more information, tools and to share your stories, please connect with me in one of the following ways.

Richard Walker

Email:
rwalker@RichardDWalker.com

Web:
RichardDWalker.com

Facebook:
facebook.com/pages/Richard-D-Walker/191522027543766

Twitter:
@WalkerRichard

Appendix: A Fully Explained Example

I can learn something from everyone I meet

The Problem: Receiving Gifts

In order to show you how this process works from start to finish, I've chosen to tackle a change that I want to make but have yet to start. The change I want to make is to not feel strange about receiving gifts from others. By 'strange' I mean that if someone does something for me, or gives me something unexpected (other than traditional times to receive gifts like birthdays or Christmas), I don't know how to accept the gift and often feel a bit negative or unsure of how to respond. Perhaps many people go through this emotion, but I feel that the way I go through it is hindering my ability to fully open up to others and to even ask for assistance in certain situations. It's not the gift itself that's the problem, whether it is an article of clothing or someone making me a meal, it's the uncertainty I feel about why the gift is being given and how I should act towards that person after receiving the gift.

While I would normally go through changes like this in my head because I'm very comfortable with this process now, I'm going to write it all out as it happens so you see an honest approach to applying the method. I won't edit my questions or answers and will use myself as a real example of a potentially emotional change.

Applying The Method

NOTE: You may want to use a "mind mapping" tool to capture and organize your thoughts (I use www.MindMeister.com). A good mind mapping tool will plot out a tree-like structure as you go helping you see the branches of your beliefs!

Step 1: Create a desire to change.

My desire to change doesn't stem from writing this book, although this is an event to tie my change to. My motivational desire stems from my past experiences with intimate relationships, family and friends. When I receive something unexpected from someone, I usually feel strange about it. To fully assess my desire to change, here are my answers to the questions about benefits and consequences.

Receiving Gifts

KEEP		CHANGE	
What Are Benefits From Behavior		*What Are Benefits From Changing*	
90	The feeling I get from receiving gifts makes me skeptical of the person giving the gift, which potentially saves me from being controlled or manipulated by the gift or the act of giving (i.e. I can't be bought).	75	I sometimes act as though I don't deserve the gift or act unappreciative because of my uncertainty, so the benefit would be acting more appropriately and making the giver feel appreciated.
50	I am awakened to the idea that I should perhaps give gifts in certain circumstances that I never considered – I become aware of a social etiquette (e.g. being invited to someone's house for dinner, it's appropriate to bring dessert or wine or something)	50	I could build stronger relationships by being able to ask others to help me
		65	I could open up more in relationships
		50	I wouldn't feel unnecessarily strange
		25	I would no longer regret how I acted when I received the gift
Who Benefits From Behavior		*Who Benefits From Changing*	
50	Those I give to as a result of learning when and why to give	50	I do
50	I do when I am perceived as being socially aware and following good social etiquette	50	The person giving to me does
240	**TOTAL**	**365**	**TOTAL**
Consequence Of Staying The Same		*Consequences Of Changing*	

I Can Change If I Want To

0	It has already affected past relationships and will continue to affect future relationships	25	Anyone that wants to help me or give something to me of their own volition
25	My future children could learn this trait from me	75	I will be happier
	What Will Happen If I Stay The Same		What Will Happen If I Change
0	If I don't change, I might learn to further deflect or suppress some of the strange behaviors, but ultimately, I'll still repeat the past experiences.	25	I will build stronger, closer relationships with others
		25	My relationships should be easier
0	I won't grow or evolve	0	I will be happier
0	I will find it increasingly harder to accept other people's efforts towards my well-being		
0	In my senior years I may reject my family based on their desire to help me if I can't help myself		
25	**TOTAL**	**150**	**TOTAL**
265	**GRAND TOTAL**	**515**	**GRAND TOTAL**

Total Points To Stay The Same = 265 vs. Total Points To Change = 515

While I was already interested in changing this attribute based on past experiences, even very recent ones, the number of reasons and related points in favor of changing clearly show that changing is in my benefit. But, it is also important to note that there are strong reasons to stay the same – roughly 1/3 of the total points are in favor of staying the same. For me, this means that there are some aspects of the behavior that I don't want to change. This result is a great indicator that I better fully define through this process what aspects I want to change and which ones I don't. I'm sure the points I don't want to change will come out in the last step as I trace through the beliefs that form my current behavior.

Step 2: Believe you can change.

Believing I can change is almost guaranteed for me because I have used this process successfully so many times in the past. But even though I know the process works, it is worth making sure I believe I can change THIS particular behavior.

Per my motivational desire to change, I know I have the strength and drive to make the change. Now, what belief do I have about this particular change? Do I simply believe I can make the change? Yes, I do. A more definitive belief would be "I believe I can change to feel good about receiving gifts when giving is appropriate". That statement captures the belief to change, how I want to change (to feel good) and qualifies the belief to keep the good parts that I already embrace (e.g. when a gift is inappropriate then I should continue to feel strange about it).

Step 3: Discover the beliefs driving your behavior.

To discover the beliefs that drive my current behavior it's time to ask myself questions and write down the answers. I'll start with the questions I listed in this book, but may ask additional questions throughout the process as I feel appropriate.

What causes me to feel strange when I get unexpected gifts?

- I'm not sure what's causing it. I think it's based on being poor as a kid and always having to do things for myself. If I wanted something I had to earn it, so when someone gives me something, I'm not sure how to feel

- I am afraid of or unsure of the person's motives when the gift is given to me
- I refuse to be controlled by anyone else
- I don't like feeling like I owe someone because they gave me a gift (as a friend once told me, friends give because they want to, not because they have to.)

How do I feel when I behave in that way?

- I feel as though I didn't earn the gift
- I question the person's motives
- My defenses rise to make sure the other person cannot control me

Who does my behavior affect?

- Myself
- The person giving the gift to me

When do I behave in the way I do?

- Whenever the gift is unexpected
- Whenever the gift is valuable (whether financially or emotionally)

Where or in what circumstances do I behave in that way?

- Usually with girlfriends
- With people who are much older than me, especially old enough to be my parent, though this happens less as I grow older

These questions and answers are the first level. Next, I will pick each answer and question it further. Note that each answer is potentially a belief that I have and by questioning that answer, I can discover if it is a core belief or the result of another belief. As I pick each answer, I'm going to now follow that answer all the way to the core belief before I move on to the next top-level answer.

Top-Level Answer - What causes me to feel strange when I get unexpected gifts?

I'm not sure what's causing it. I think it's based on being poor as a kid and always having to do things for myself. If I wanted something I had to earn it, so when someone gives me something, I'm not sure how to feel.

1. When I was poor, how did I feel about getting a gift?

    a. As a little kid, under age 10, I was elated! I loved getting things.

    b. As an older kid, over age 10, I had learned to be afraid of why I was getting the gift.

        i. I'm not sure, but I feel like adults or teenagers who wanted the kids out of their way so they could do drugs, might have used gifts from time to time to get my brother and I out of the way and to shield us from their drug use.

        ii. My father bought us gifts when we came to visit him, but wasn't really there for us emotionally, so in some ways I felt like we were being bought.

            1. When my brother, sister and I visited my dad, he would give us toys so we could play quietly while he slept or did whatever it was he did.

- a. I may believe that receiving a gift means that someone is trying to 'buy' me or get me out of their way
- c. I remember a time that I was reprimanded for being aggressive about getting a gift. My mom's boyfriend bought three toy boats: one for his little son, one for my brother and one for me. When he brought the first one out, being the oldest and biggest I fought the other two off to get it first. Then I saw the other two boats, which I considered to be better than mine and I was told that because I was so greedy that I was now stuck with my choice! I felt punished for how I handled getting that gift.
    - i. Am I afraid that getting a gift is going to result in feeling reprimanded?
        1. Not really.
    - ii. Do I think accepting a gift makes me greedy?
        1. No, I don't feel that way.
- d. When I graduated college and was really poor, my mentor took me shopping at Brooks Brothers and bought me a suit (worth $500). I didn't immediately thank him, and I'm not sure why. I had to be reminded to thank him for the gift. It was very rude of me.
    - i. That was a good learning experience for me and I have learned that lesson.
    - ii. Why was I so slow to say thank you?
        1. I think part of it was that I felt my mentor was really wealthy and could easily afford it.

       a. Just because he could afford it didn't make the gift any less thoughtful or caring. Wealth, and the ability that comes with it, does not make you less caring.
    2. I may have thought that I did thank him without saying it.
2. How does having to earn things for myself make me feel strange when I don't have to earn it? Shouldn't I feel even happier to accept the gift?
    a. Logically, I do feel that I should be happy to get something without working for it given how hard I have worked for everything I have.
    b. My pride in making my own accomplishments is very high.
       i. I have learned that I can't do everything on my own, so I no longer have to feel that I have to do everything in order to feel pride for my accomplishments (part of the accomplishment is getting others to believe in me and help out, and they share in the reward too)
    c. If I can't afford the gift with my own money, I don't feel I should have it.
       i. Being poor made me feel left out of what others had or were able to do (like vacations, clothes, cars, toys, food, etc)
          1. I am no longer poor, and I have experienced having more money than I need (I owned

my dream car, traveled outside the US, have nice clothes, etc) so this no longer applies.

 ii. When someone buys me something of high value that I can't afford today,

  1. and they can afford to do it, then they are doing it because they want to and I won't let that action cause me to feel strange.

  2. and they cannot afford to do it, then they are doing it to control me in some manner OR they have their own problems to overcome, neither of which I will allow to control me.

d. When I was little I felt jealous of other kids who got things that their family could afford and mine could not. When someone gave me those 'things', I was happy and willing to accept the gift, including when my mom's boss paid for my trip to Florida with the marching band when we couldn't afford it.

e. When I got to college and saw kids with really expensive things (e.g. Ferraris, vacation homes, etc), I no longer got jealous I got cynical.

 i. I felt that they didn't deserve their 'things'

  1. If I received something valuable that I couldn't afford, then I would be just like them and not deserve it.

   a. I may believe that receiving gifts makes me like a spoiled brat and less deserving of the possession

  ii. I felt that having those things made those kids jerks or less of the people I wanted to be around.

    1. As a result of not wanting to be how I perceived those kids were, I didn't want to receive things I didn't deserve.

      a. I may believe that receiving gifts makes me like a spoiled brat and less deserving of the possession

  iii. Those kids didn't appreciate the opportunities and things they had but had not done anything to get

    1. I wanted to always appreciate things I had, so I had to earn my things in order to feel like I appreciate them.

      a. I may believe that receiving a gift means that I won't appreciate its value or worth

Top-Level Answer - What causes me to feel strange when I get unexpected gifts?

I am afraid or unsure of the person's motives when giving the gift to me.

1. What causes me to feel unsure of another person's motives?

  a. When the person is aggressive in how they try to attract my attention overall, I'm leery of the reason why they're giving me a gift.

    i. I feel they may be trying to 'buy' my attention or affection and that the gift comes with expectations that I don't want to be beholden to

1. I may believe that receiving a gift means that someone is trying to 'buy' me
   b. When the person can't afford the gift they're giving, I feel bad that they would give it to me.
      i. I don't want the other person to be put in a difficult position just to give me something
         1. As a kid I became aware of how poor we were and didn't want my mom spending money on me when it wasn't necessary.
            a. Spending money on the wrong things meant stress and unhappiness for other things (which is why I probably don't care about clothes as much as I care about other things – I don't need the nicest clothing, but I do need good food)
               i. I may believe that receiving a gift causes the giver undue stress and unhappiness
      ii. I don't want the other person to spend money and be stressed out as a result because I don't want to deal with the stress they caused themselves as a result.
         1. I may believe that receiving a gift causes the giver undue stress and unhappiness
      iii. I don't like 'guilt-trips' that others deliver after they buy something that costs a lot and isn't quite what I wanted or needed, and didn't ask for in the first place

1. I may believe that I should feel guilty if someone gives me something because I didn't do something for them.

Top-Level Answer - What causes me to feel strange when I get unexpected gifts?

I refuse to be controlled by anyone else

1. I have been manipulated by other people when they have done something for me or given me something that I didn't expect.
    a. Since I refuse to be controlled by anyone else, I may reject the gift because I see it as an attempt to control me.
        i. I may believe that receiving a gift is an attempt to control me
2. I don't like it when people feel like they owe me if I give them a gift
    a. Because I don't like to be controlled, I don't want others to feel like I might be trying to control them when I give a gift.
        i. I may believe that giving a gift is an attempt to control someone else

Top-Level Answer - What causes me to feel strange when I get unexpected gifts?

I don't like feeling like I owe someone because they gave me a gift

1. If an acquaintance gives me a Christmas gift, I feel like I should give them one in return.

a. As an adult, I have overcome this particular scenario to a large degree
2. I can't think of an instance where I still feel like I owe someone (in a negative way) if they give me a gift I didn't expect.

Top-Level Answer - How do I feel when I behave in that way?

I feel as though I didn't earn the gift

1. This feeling was addressed earlier.

Top-Level Answer - How do I feel when I behave in that way?

I question the person's motives

1. This feeling was addressed earlier.

Top-Level Answer - How do I feel when I behave in that way?

My defenses rise to make sure the other person cannot control me

1. This feeling was addressed earlier.

Top-Level Answer - When do I behave in the way I do?

Whenever the gift is unexpected

1. This feeling was addressed earlier.

Top-Level Answer - When do I behave in the way I do?

Whenever the gift is valuable (whether financially or emotionally)

1. This feeling was addressed earlier.

Top-Level Answer - Where or in what circumstances do I behave in that way?

Usually with girlfriends

1. My first long-term girlfriend was very manipulative and almost everything she did for me had a built-in debt.

a. I felt guilty about my earliest girlfriends doing things for me, especially when we became intimate.

   i. My friends that were girls all confided in me their sense of guilt related to intimacy, so when I became intimate with a girl, I didn't want to make that girl feel the way my friends had expressed they felt.

      1. I probably learned many of my own behaviors from my mom because I have always closely identified with my mother, but I cannot think of any specific instances where I learned a particular trait.

         a. I no longer feel that intimacy creates a debt between two people and don't feel that this is a problem for me now.

2. My long-term relationships before age 27 were full of manipulation and the sense of owing whenever someone did something for me.

   a. My relationships as I entered my 30's were more mature and manipulation in negative forms was not successful from my perspective because I recognized it and stopped it before it had an impact.

   b. I still fear that a girl's motives for doing something for me comes with 'strings attached'

      i. I need to be able to assess whether there are strings attached or not in order to feel ok about receiving a gift

         1. I may have given girls more in the way of gifts than I should have in the past in order

             to ensure that no strings were attached from me to them

    a. I don't have to over-give in order to prove there are no strings attached.

  ii. I want to be able to accept gifts even when strings are attached without feeling guilty or a sense of obligation

    1. It is not my fault that the strings are attached

       a. I cannot control anyone else's motives for why they give

    2. I can be deserving of gifts, so I don't have to assume there are expectations tied to it

    3. I like giving gifts and I don't expect anything in return, so I can extend the same benefit to the giver

    4. I don't ask for, nor demand gifts, so if the girl expects something in return, that is something she needs to work on in the relationship, not me.

Top-Level Answer - Where or in what circumstances do I behave in that way?

With people who are much older than me, especially old enough to be my parent, though this happens less as I grow older

  1. This circumstance has not occurred in at least five years.

What Are My Core Beliefs?

As I scan over all the statements I wrote, I need to pick out the lowest-level statements that pertain to my beliefs. You can probably see that many of the things I wrote are beliefs, some limiting and some empowering the behavior I want. I have also made note of beliefs that I have already dealt with and changed or overcame, but because I haven't made changes to enough of the beliefs, the overall change has not occurred. Changing only one or a few beliefs in a set of many beliefs and expecting to have a different behavior is like taking down one sail on a ship with multiple sails and expecting the ship to stop. The ship hasn't stopped, although it has probably slowed down a little.

The beliefs I believe to be the root causes of my current behavior, are as follows:

1. I may believe that receiving a gift means that someone is trying to 'buy' me
2. I may believe that receiving gifts makes me like a spoiled brat and less deserving of the possession
3. I may believe that receiving a gift means that I won't appreciate its value or worth
4. I may believe that receiving a gift causes the giver undue stress and unhappiness
5. I may believe that I should feel guilty if someone gives me something because I didn't do something for them.
6. I may believe that receiving a gift is an attempt to control me
7. I may believe that giving a gift is an attempt to control someone else

There are other beliefs that probably could be inferred from everything I wrote, but I believe these seven are the ones that I need to assess in order to make a change.

Step 4: Choose beliefs that will create the desired behavior.

In this last step, I will now review each belief and ask myself three questions to determine whether to keep or change the belief:

1. What is the most effective belief for me?
2. How will changing the belief affect my other behaviors?
3. Do I want to change the belief?

1. **I may believe that receiving a gift means that someone is trying to 'buy' me**

    More Effective Belief: I believe that receiving a gift is a gesture of generosity and a way for someone to tell me they care for me.

    How will changing the belief affect me? If I assume that someone is giving me a gift for positive reasons, then I won't feel negative about their gesture, nor will I offend them with my reaction. If their motive turns out to be negative, I know I have the communication skills to deal with that situation if it arises.

    Do I want to change the belief? Yes.

2. **I may believe that receiving gifts makes me like a spoiled brat and less deserving of the possession**

    More Effective Belief: I believe that receiving a gift makes me lucky and cherished by the person giving the gift.

    How will changing the belief affect me? I will feel good about getting the gift and not wonder if I'm going to be spoiled (especially since I'm an adult and no longer a child that can be spoiled).

Do I want to change the belief? Yes

3. **I may believe that receiving a gift means that I won't appreciate its value or worth**

More Effective Belief: I believe that receiving a gift gives me an even higher appreciation of the value of the gift because it came from someone else's effort, which is worth more than my own.

How will changing the belief affect me? I will show my appreciation for receiving gifts more quickly and freely. I will treat the gift with the same care I treat for the things I earned on my own.

Do I want to change the belief? Yes

4. **I may believe that receiving a gift causes the giver undue stress and unhappiness**

More Effective Belief: I believe that the person giving the gift truly wants to give or they wouldn't do it.

How will changing the belief affect me? I don't need to worry about the stress or unhappiness of someone who is freely giving a gift to me.

Do I want to change the belief? Yes

5. **I may believe that I should feel guilty if someone gives me something because I didn't do something for them.**

More Effective Belief: I believe that I should show the person giving the gift my appreciation and value for their efforts.

How will changing the belief affect me? I don't have to feel obligated or guilty for receiving a gift if I show the person giving the gift how much I appreciate it (they didn't give me the gift to get a gift in return, they wanted me to be happy so if I show my happiness I don't owe them anything else).

Do I want to change the belief? Yes

6. **I may believe that receiving a gift is an attempt to control me**

   More Effective Belief: I believe that a gift that is given freely is meant to make my life better.

   How will changing the belief affect me? I won't second-guess another person's motives unless they show that their gift wasn't given freely, at which point I will rely on my communication skills to work through that situation.

   Do I want to change the belief? Yes

7. **I may believe that giving a gift is an attempt to control someone else**

   More Effective Belief: I believe that I only give gifts because I want to give to someone and because they deserve the gift.

   How will changing the belief affect me? I won't limit my ability to give to others nor contradict how I feel when I receive a gift from someone else.

   Do I want to change the belief? Yes

How And Why The Change Will Be Permanent

As I mentioned in the last chapter, a change will become permanent when the habits and thought processes related to these beliefs are finally changed. Using this process to change I have proven that I have both the desire and belief to change. I have also assessed what may be causing the behavior by looking for the root causes and core beliefs, some of which stem back to my early childhood. Finally, by reviewing each core belief I have decided which ones to change (all of them in this case), what new belief to adopt and why I should adopt it. The only step left is to be aware of the times when the old belief appears and immediately replace it with the new belief.

It is interesting to me how much being poor has affected my life, and I suppose some reader will think I'm way too focused on that aspect. The reality is many of our behaviors really do result from circumstances and situations we experienced early on. We probably all know people who grew up wealthy and have just as many issues to resolve as anyone else. The important thing isn't what we went through, but how we think and what we believe about what we went through.

You'll discover in going through this process that simply identifying your beliefs and new ones to use will make immediate changes in your behavior. Of course any habits that exist will have to be broken down, but your mind will already be absorbing the new beliefs and putting them to use. In just the few hours it took me to write this chapter, I already feel some clouds have lifted. I still have to go through a few events of receiving gifts to fully know how this change will work however I am comforted to know I have a new set of beliefs to use when the events arise. I feel empowered to face a challenge I didn't know how to deal with until now.

There are two major reasons why this change will be permanent. The first one is because I have the desire to make the change, which will push me to break the habits when they occur. The second one is because this process helped me fully comprehend the beliefs that form my current reality allowing me to choose different beliefs that will form the reality I want. This process laid a solid foundation in which to anchor my thoughts and habits, a foundation that won't be easily changed or moved. Inherently, by going through this process, you will create a long-lasting change that will only be changed when you choose to modify your beliefs again. Plus, if you write down your beliefs, you'll have your own custom reference guide to your reality.

About The Author

Richard Walker has overcome a lifetime of childhood challenges: from his father becoming a drug and alcohol addict, to living on welfare with his two siblings and single mother, to moving and switching schools every 9 to 18 months, to working 35 hours per week to pay for his education while attending the University of Southern California as a full-time student.

Through these challenges he learned to choose happiness and see opportunities for success. Starting his first company at age 12, Richard is a serial entrepreneur and innovator. As the CEO and co-founder of Efficient Technology Inc, he designs enterprise solutions for Fortune 500 companies, which currently result in saving over three trees every day in paper reductions.

Richard resides in Redondo Beach, California with his fiancé and enjoys writing, public speaking, painting, surfing, snowboarding and travelling. Find out more at his website and blog.

Richard D. Walker

Email:
rwalker@RichardDWalker.com

Web:
RichardDWalker.com

Facebook:
facebook.com/pages/Richard-D-Walker/191522027543766

Twitter:
@WalkerRichard

Blog:
EfficientCEO.com

LaVergne, TN USA
07 March 2011
219173LV00001B/10/P